creative
DOUGHCRAFT

creative
DOUGHCRAFT

Patricia Hughes

Guild of Master Craftsman Publications Ltd

First published 1999 by
Guild of Master Craftsman Publications Ltd,
166 High Street, Lewes,
East Sussex, BN7 1XU

ISBN 1 86108 122 7

Photographs by Anthony Bailey
Cover photography by Anthony Bailey
Black-and-white line drawings by John Yates

A catalogue record for this book
is available from the British Library

Designed by Teresa Dearlove
Cover designed by Wheelhouse Design

Typeface: Frutiger
Colour origination by Viscan Graphics, Singapore.
Printed and bound by Kyodo Printing, Singapore, under the
supervision of MRM Graphics, Winslow, Buckinghamshire, UK.

Contents

Acknowledgements

To my husband Anthony – without his encouragement and support this book would never have been written.

With thanks to my daughters Amanda and Natalie, for accepting my first dough models with gratitude, and my sisters Isabel, Rosemary and Mary, who listened to me endlessly talking about dough, dough and dough.

Many thanks to Catering Compliments, 22 Market Buildings, Maidstone, Kent ME14 1HP, for supplying all the necessary tools and equipment.

My thanks to Hawthorne Hill, Unit 3, Milvale Studios, Milvale Street, Middleport, Stoke-on-Trent ST6 3NT, for supplying a sugarcraft cutter.

Introduction

The first time I saw a doughcraft model was in an art and craft shop. I couldn't believe that flour, salt and water could create such wonderful things.

I didn't think I could ever make a dough model good enough to hang on a wall. I later found a book on salt dough and started experimenting. When I made my first model I thought that I would not want to show it to anyone, but by the time I finished painting and varnishing it, I couldn't wait to show it off to my family.

Working with dough is therapeutic and relaxing. As you progress from simple dough models and move on to more complex projects you will become hooked. I hope that the projects in this book will spur you on to experiment with salt dough, so you create your own unique style. I would thoroughly recommend doughcraft to anyone wishing to surprise themselves with a talent they never thought they possessed.

Good luck with all your projects, and remember, practice makes perfect – so persevere and you will be rewarded.

Chapter 1
Tools and materials

You will already have the necessary tools and materials to make and model dough in your kitchen: plain flour, table salt, water, a rolling pin and a small knife. As you progress, you may find that you want to buy the odd flower or leaf cutter to create a special dough model, but you will be surprised how many useful gadgets you already have in your kitchen cupboards.

Basic equipment

It is worth getting together a basic kit of equipment.
These are things you will need for most dough projects,
so they are not mentioned in the equipment list at the
beginning of each project.

Mixing bowl, wooden spoon and fork, to mix the dough
Large and small rolling pins, for rolling out dough
Small sharp knife, for cutting the dough into pieces
Non-stick baking tray
A range of small paintbrushes, for smoothing dough,
and applying glue, varnish and paint
Ruler

Useful tools and equipment

- Drinking straws, for making holes
- Garlic press, for making long strands of dough, ideal for grass or hair
- Florist's wire, for making stems for flowers and leaves
- Cocktail sticks, for making holes in dough, positioning small parts, and supporting joined pieces of dough
- Modelling tools, for making flowers and providing undulating edges
- Small scissors, for cutting the edges of dough, i.e. fringes and small shapes
- Tweezers, for positioning small pieces of dough, i.e. pushing stamens into the centre of flowers
- Strong hairpins, to make hooks
- Wire cutters, for cutting and bending wire
- Strong wire, for making hanging loops
- Beads, for the eyes of figures and adding decoration to mobiles

Pastry or cookie cutters

These are available from most department stores, supermarkets and hardware stores in a variety of shapes – round, square, fluted, hearts, Christmas decorations, numbers, letters, animals, fruit, flower shapes and leaves.

Special cutters and modelling tools are also available from sugarcraft shops who supply many varieties of flower and leaf cutters and moulds to make more complex shapes like birds and butterflies.

Chapter 2
Salt dough

The materials needed to make salt dough are cheap and readily available – flour, salt and water – so you can afford to experiment.

Making salt dough

225g (8oz) plain flour
100g (4oz) table salt
100ml (4fl oz or ½ cup) water

Method

 Mix together the flour and salt in a mixing bowl. Add water and bind the mixture together with a fork.

 Scoop the mixture into a ball with your hands and begin kneading it. If the mixture feels too wet, add more flour, or add a little more water, a drip at a time, if it is too dry.

 Continue kneading the dough for about 10 to 15 minutes. Poorly kneaded dough will crack when baked.

 Wrap the dough in plastic wrap or cling film to prevent it from drying out. The dough will keep fresh for a day.

 Once you have shaped the salt dough, place the finished item onto an ovenproof sheet or baking tray.

Baking salt dough

Salt dough models should be baked at temperatures of between 100°C–120°C (200°F–250°F or Gas Mark ¼–½). Any hotter than this and the dough will dry on the outside, but stay damp on the inside. If you find that the dough is baking too quickly, move it to a lower shelf in the oven and reduce the temperature slightly.

The amount of time it takes to bake a salt dough model will depend on the model's size and thickness. As a general guide it takes approximately one hour for every 6mm (¼in) of dough thickness to bake.

Each project in this book has a suggested baking time. To make sure that the dough is baked, turn the dough over and give it a gentle tap in the centre, it should sound hollow. If it gives a dull sound return it to the oven for more baking.

All ovens vary, and as you become familiar with baking salt dough, you will find a suitable temperature for your oven.

It is worth remembering that the salt in dough will turn metal objects, like cutters and uncoated baking trays, rusty unless they are washed immediately after use.

Problems with cracking

The two most common causes of cracking are:
- dough which hasn't been kneaded sufficiently,
- dough which has been baked at too high a temperature. If the oven is set too high, the dough will swell on the inside, causing it to crack.

Rapid temperature changes will cause cracks. To be on the safe side, allow the dough to cool down gradually by leaving it in the oven with the heat turned off after baking. This way, the dough will have time to adjust to a cooler temperature.

Cracks will sometimes appear hours after the dough has been baked. If this happens, just fill in the cracks with some fresh dough, but do not return the dough to the oven for further baking. Leave the dough to air dry for a few hours. When the dough is completely dry, sand the filled-in cracks smooth with fine sandpaper.

A salt dough model that has been kept in a damp atmosphere will almost certainly have become wet. To test if the dough is wet, give it a gentle squeeze to see if it feels soft and pliable. If the model is wet, place it in a warm dry place, like an airing cupboard, and leave it for a few days until it has dried out.

Finishing salt dough

If you don't want to paint your dough model, but want to give it a golden brown finish, beat an egg with one tablespoon of water, and brush it onto the raw dough before baking. Repeat this every process every half hour whilst the dough is being baked. The more egg glaze you use, the deeper the final colour will be.

Painting

You can use many different types of paint on salt dough, all of which are available from art and craft shops.

Poster paint produces bright colours but can dry powdery.

Watercolours come in small tubes and are easy to use.

Gouache is sold in small tubes. They can be used to make an opaque block of colour, or watered down to give a gentle wash.

Acrylic paints can be used, but have a rather shiny finish, like plastic, when dry.

The more time you spend painting your model, the better the result will be. If you smudge the paint, use a damp cotton bud to erase the smudge immediately. Allow plenty of time for the paint to dry before varnishing over it.

You can colour salt dough by adding paint to the raw dough, but you won't be able to bake the dough afterwards, or rather, if you do you will find that the colours turn very dark. Coloured salt dough should be air-dried so that the colours stay fresh and bright.

Varnishing

Salt dough is extremely vulnerable to moisture, so it is essential to apply at least two coats of clear gloss oil-based polyurethane varnish. Yacht varnish is a strong sealant which can be used on larger models. Make sure you cover all the small nooks and crannies. Keep a brush solely for varnishing and always clean it afterwards in white spirit (mineral spirit), turpentine or a turpentine substitute.

Chapter 3
Bread dough

Bread dough has a wonderfully fine texture which allows you to create delicate shapes, like flowers, leaves, butterflies and angel wings. It can be coloured before modelling by adding water-based paints to the dough.

Making bread dough

100g (4oz) white bread, without the crusts
1 tablespoon white acrylic paint (available from DIY stores)
3 tablespoons PVA glue (available from art and craft shops)
1 teaspoon glycerine or glycerol (available from chemists)

Method

 Break or cut the bread into small pieces and place them in an old mixing bowl. Add the paint, glue and glycerine or glycerol and bind the mixture together with a fork.

 Scoop up the mixture and squeeze it together. It will be a sticky mess, but don't worry, this is normal. Continue squeezing the mixture for about 15 minutes, and you will gradually notice that your hands become cleaner. You will then be able to knead the dough.

 Keep kneading until you have a soft ball of white dough. Kneading the dough thoroughly will help to prevent cracking.

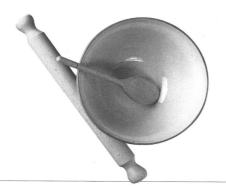

Drying bread dough

Wrap the dough in plastic wrap or cling film until you are ready to use it. Rubbing a little hand cream on your hands before you start will help to stop the dough from sticking to your fingers.

Bread dough will keep for up to three months if wrapped in plastic wrap or cling film, placed in an air-tight container and stored in a refrigerator.

Bread dough is not baked, so it does not crack (provided that it has been well kneaded), it is simply left to air-dry for approximately eight hours.

- The finished models will shrink slightly during drying, but this will hardly be noticeable.
- Thin objects which are left to dry on a flat surface must be turned frequently to stop the sides from curling upwards.

Finishing bread dough

Bread dough can be coloured before it is modelled, saving a lot of time and effort. When the coloured dough is dry, you can also paint over it, adding spots, stripes or decoration of your choice.

An easier way to colour dough is to place the dough between a piece of plastic wrap or cling film, this way you will not waste any of the paint or get paint all over your hands.

Colouring bread dough

 Flatten a small piece of dough on a work surface, and put some paint in the centre of the dough.

Fold the edges of the dough together and gently press the paint into the dough. Don't press too firmly or the paint will ooze out at the sides and you will end up with more paint on your fingers than on the dough.

 Knead the dough until you have obtained an even colour throughout. Wrap each colour separately in plastic wrap or cling film to prevent it from drying out.

Remember that the paint is very rich in colour, so only use a small amount at first. If you find that the colour isn't deep enough, add more paint. If the colour is too rich, add more white dough.

Varnishing bread dough

Although bread dough isn't as susceptible to damp and moisture as salt dough, it still needs to be varnished. Use clear acrylic varnish (available in most art and craft shops). It is completely transparent and does not yellow with age. Give your dough model two coats of varnish, making sure that the first coat is completely dry before applying the next. Use a separate brush for varnishing and clean it after use.

Chapter 4
Basic techniques

Joining dough together is a simple technique which you will need to use again and again. Try practising on simple shapes, concentrating on achieving a smooth finish which will hold firmly.

Joining salt dough together

Wet one side of the join. Don't put too much water on the brush, or the dough will get slippery and the pieces will be difficult to join. Gently push the two pieces of dough together and leave the joint to dry.

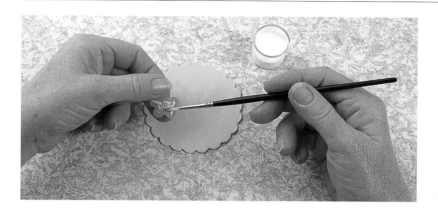

Joining bread dough together

Bread dough can be joined together using PVA glue, which dries clear. Put some glue on one side of the join and gently press the two pieces together. Leave the joint to dry.

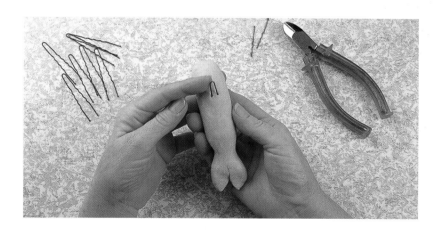

Hooks and hangings

If you are going to make a dough model to hang on a wall, it will need a hook. There are several things that can be used to make hooks, e.g. wire or paperclips. Strong hairpins work best. Cut off the ends of the hairpin with wire cutters and trim the rounded ends to about 25mm (1in). Just jab the hook into the back of the dough before it is baked or dried. Make sure that you stick the hook in fairly deep and put it in a place where it cannot be seen.

Chapter 5
Making simple shapes

These simple shapes will feature in the projects to come.
There are lots of basic shapes which you can make to enhance
your dough models. Adding a bow or flower here and there
will turn your piece into something really special.

Making bows

 Roll out some dough and cut three strips the same length as each other and one slightly longer strip.

 Join two of the shorter strips together at an angle to form the dangling ends of the bow. Cut the joined ends into a point and cut a notch into the loose ends.

 Take the longer strip and fold each end under towards the back. This strip will form the main part of the bow.

 Wrap the remaining shorter strip around the middle of the bow, joining it at the back. Join the bow to the notched strips.

Making frills

 Roll out some dough until it is about 3mm (⅛in) thick.

 Stamp out a circle using a 75mm (3in) fluted cutter. Remove a smaller circle from the inside of the one you have cut with a 25mm (1in) round cutter.

 Using the cocktail stick as a mini rolling pin, roll the end of the stick from side to side, making grooves in between each flute.

 Work your way around the circle until all of the flutes have been rolled. Then, cut the frilled circle to the length required.

Weaving dough

 Roll out some dough to about 3mm-6mm (⅛in–¼in) on your work surface. Cut the dough into 13mm (½in) wide strips.

 Take two strips and lay one vertical and the other horizontal to form a cross.

 Keep adding alternate vertical and horizontal strips, weaving them under and over each other as you go.

 Continue to add strips until you have a piece of woven dough of the right size for the project you are doing.

Making twists

 Roll two finger-sized ropes of dough of about the same length and thickness.

 Starting from the centre, twist the two pieces together. Try not to lift the dough, keep it resting on the surface to stop it from stretching.

 Once the twist is completed, trim the ends with the knife, and secure with a little water.

Making leaves

You can buy cutters in a variety of leaf shapes and sizes. Using a cutter to make leaves is simple. Just roll out the dough and use the cutter to stamp out leaf shapes. Your cutter may also add veins to the leaf, if not add these with a small knife.

You can also make leaves by hand, ensuring that each leaf is unique.

 Roll a pencil thin rope of dough about 50mm (2in) long.

 Taper one end of each rope with your finger and thumb.

Making corn

 Holding the tapered end of the rope, use a small pair of scissors to make small snips in the dough, starting at the top and working your way around and down the rope.

Making flowers

There is a wide variety of cutters available in flower shapes, but making your own flowers can be satisfying. Use your own garden and favourite flowers for inspiration.

Roses

Roll a tiny rope of dough in the palm of your hand. Flatten the rope out and curl it into a bud.

Roll a pea-size ball of dough and press it between your finger and thumb to make a petal shape. Wrap the petal around the bud.

Using a little more dough, make another slightly larger petal and wrap it around the first petal.

Make another three petals in the same way. Make sure each one is slightly larger than the last, wrapping them around the previous petal.

Five or six petals are usually enough to make a rose, but you can add more petals according to the size of rose you want.

Rose buds

Make a small rose, but instead of opening the petals, close them gently with your finger and thumb. Add two small leaves. Snip the top of the leaves and wrap them around the bud.

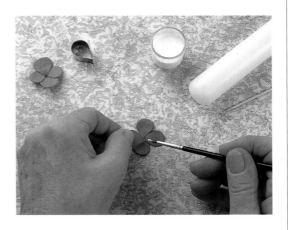

Pansies

Roll out some dough so that it is quite thin. Cut out four leaves with a medium-size cutter. Flatten the round end of the leaf between your finger and thumb.

The stalk end of the leaf will become the petal stem. Join the petals together to make a flower.

Make a hole in the centre of the flower with a cocktail stick.

If you want to add an extra touch to your flowers, buy some decorative stamens. These are available from sugarcraft and catering outlets.

1
Toy
garland

A simple circular garland base is decorated with a collection of colourful and fun toys. This item would make an ideal gift for a child. The base of the garland is made from salt dough. The tiny toys are made using bread dough which was coloured with paint.
Actual size: 150mm (6in) in diameter

Making the garland

Salt dough

225g (8oz) plain flour

100g (4oz) salt

100ml (4fl oz or ½ cup) water

You will need:

Large hole drinking straw

230mm (9in) ribbon

100mm (4in) strong wire for hanging the garland

White, blue and yellow paints

Varnish

 Roll a thick rope of salt dough, about 90mm (3½in) in diameter. Cut the rope to 510mm (20in) and flatten it with the palm of your hand.

 Trim the two ends of the rope with a knife and join them together to form a circle with a little water. Make a hole either side of the join using the drinking straw.

 Bake the garland shape at 120°C (250°F or Gas Mark ½) for about four hours.

Making the toys

Bread dough

50g (2oz) white bread without the crusts

½ tablespoon of white acrylic paint

1½ tablespoons of PVA glue

½ level teaspoon of glycerine or glycerol

•

Divide the dough into five pieces and colour them purple, pink, yellow, blue and green (see page 10). Wrap the colours separately in plastic wrap or cling film.

You will need:

Small blossom cutter

Small and medium-size heart cutter

Small leaf cutter

Cocktail stick

Fine-mesh tea strainer

Outer cover of a ballpoint pen

Purple, pink, yellow, blue and green paints

Snail

 Roll a thin rope, 100mm (4in) long, from pink dough. Roll a slightly shorter rope of yellow dough and attach it to the pink rope. Flatten and curl the combined rope to make the body.

 Make the head from a small pink dough ball. Make the eyes with the end of a cocktail stick, and roll a small blue dough ball to make the nose.

 Make the hat from a small ball of flattened yellow dough. Roll a tiny blue dough ball to make the pompom.

 Flatten a small piece of yellow dough. Cut a small blossom with the cutter and join it to the front of the body.

Doll

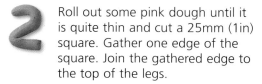

1. Make the legs from two thin ropes of yellow dough 25mm (1in) long. Join the two ropes together at the top. Make the shoes from two tiny balls of green dough.

2. Roll out some pink dough until it is quite thin and cut a 25mm (1in) square. Gather one edge of the square. Join the gathered edge to the top of the legs.

3. Make the arms by rolling yellow dough into two thin ropes 13mm (½in) long. Roll two tiny balls of green dough for the hands and attach them to the arms. Join the arms either side of the dress.

4. Make the head from a small marble-size ball of yellow dough and join it to the top of the dress. Make the eyes and mouth with the end of a cocktail stick. Roll a small pink ball for the nose.

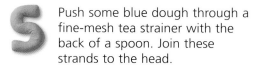

5. Push some blue dough through a fine-mesh tea strainer with the back of a spoon. Join these strands to the head.

6. Make a pocket from pink dough and join it to the front of the dress and leave the finished doll to dry.

Train

 1 Roll out some blue dough until it is 13mm (½in) thick. Cut a 13mm x 50mm (½in x 2in) rectangle.

 2 Roll a thick rope of yellow dough and cut 25mm (1in) for the front of the train. Make the funnels from green dough.

 3 Roll out a small piece of blue dough and cut out a small heart shape using a cutter. Join it to the side of the train.

 4 Cut some thick blue dough, 13mm x 25mm (½in x 1in), and join it to the end of the rope.

 5 Make the body and arms of the driver from small ropes. Make the head from a small ball and join it to the body. Make holes for the eyes with a cocktail stick.

 6 Cut out four small circles using the wide end of the pen cover to make the wheels and the driver's hat.

 7 Roll a tiny ball for the driver's nose, and one for the top of the hat.

House

1. Roll out some purple dough until it is quite thin. Cut a 25mm (1in) square to make the main part of the house.

2. Roll some yellow dough to the same thickness and cut out the roof. Cut out two hearts from flattened pink dough for the windows.

3. Cut a small door and chimney from rolled-out green dough. Roll out a piece of blue dough and cut out a blossom using the cutter. Join this to the roof.

Boat

1. Roll out a piece of green dough and cut out a 6mm x 25mm (¼in x 1in) rectangle.

2. Trim off two corners and make three circles with the pointed end of the pen cover.

3. Make the sail by cutting a triangle, 25mm (1in) wide and high, from rolled-out yellow dough.

4. Join the sail to the boat and make a vertical mark in the sail with the knife.

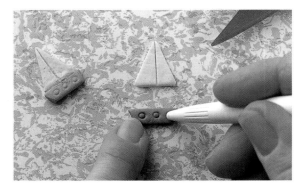

Duck

 Make the body from a small ball of purple dough and pinch one side to form a tail.

 Roll a small ball of purple dough for the head and join it to the body. Make the eye with the end of a cocktail stick.

 Cut a wing from pink dough using a leaf cutter. Cut out a blossom from yellow dough using a cutter and attach it to the top of the head to make a hat.

 Make a small beak from yellow dough and join it to the head.

Dinosaur

 Roll a small ball of green dough and flatten it slightly. Pinch out one side to form the tail. Snip notches on one side to make the spines on the back and tail.

 Make a leg from a tiny green dough rope. Make the head from a small flattened green dough ball. Make small snips on the side of the head, to follow the spines down the back and tail.

 Make a hole for the eye with the end of a cocktail stick.

 Cut a thin oblong shape from rolled-out blue dough to make the bow. Roll a tiny yellow ball for the centre of the bow. Join it to the body.

Rocking horse

 Roll a thin pink dough rope and flatten it to make the rocker. Decorate it with small circles made with a pen cover.

 Roll out some purple dough and cut out the shape of a horse. Don't worry too much if the shape is not perfect, as the tail and mane will hide most of it.

 Make the saddle from a tiny circle of green dough. Add a tiny pink ball to the top of the saddle and decorate it using the pen cover.

 Push some yellow dough through the fine-mesh tea strainer with the back of a wooden spoon to make thin strands for the tail and mane. Join these to the horse.

 Make a small ear from purple dough and join it to the head. Make the eye with the end of a cocktail stick.

 When the horse is dry, add the bridle with green paint using a fine paintbrush.

Finishing the garland

After the garland has cooled, paint it white. When the white paint layer is dry, add blue and yellow paint dots. When the paint is completely dry, apply two coats of varnish.

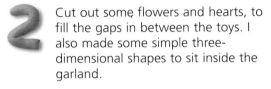

Cut out some flowers and hearts, to fill the gaps in between the toys. I also made some simple three-dimensional shapes to sit inside the garland.

Arrange the toys on the garland and glue them in place. When the glue is dry they can be varnished.

Thread wire through the holes in the top of the garland, twisting the two ends at the back to form a hanging loop. Thread the ribbon in the front of the wire and tie it in a bow.

2
Sunflower garland

This bright, cheerful garland is delightful but simple to make. The garland itself is a rope, joined at one end. Thin strands of salt dough are wrapped around it to give a straw-like effect. The petals of the sunflowers and leaf decoration are made using simple leaf cutters. The finished project is finished with a colourful ribbon, which covers the hanging hook.

Actual size: 190mm (7½in) diameter

Salt dough
340g (12oz) plain flour
150g (6oz) salt
150ml (6fl oz or ¾ cup) water

You will need:
Drinking straw with a large hole
Large leaf cutter
Medium-size leaf cutter
Cocktail stick
Strong wire, 100mm (4in), to make a hanging hook
Ribbon, 380mm (15in)
Red, yellow, green and brown paints of your choice

Making the garland

1 Roll a thick rope of dough about 90mm (3½in) in diameter and 560mm (22in) long. Trim the two ends and join them together to make a circle. Flatten the circle with the palm of your hand.

 2 Place the circle on a baking tray. Make two holes in the circle, one either side of the join.

 3 Roll out a thin strand about 100mm (4in) long. Wet the ends of the strand with water and wrap the strand around the garland tucking the ends around the back.

 4 Continue rolling and wrapping thin strands around the garland until the surface is covered. Don't cover the holes at the top of the garland.

Making the sunflower and leaf decoration

 Roll out some salt dough so it is about 3mm (⅛in) thick. Using the large leaf cutter, cut out 18 leaf shapes. Mark out the veins of the leaves. Arrange the leaves along the bottom of the circle, to create a background for the sunflowers.

 Roll out some more dough. Using the medium-size leaf cutter, cut out 12 leaves to make the petals of the sunflower. Cut approximately 6mm (¼in) off the base of each leaf and join them together in a circle at the bottom of the garland.

 Cut another eight leaves, snipping off their stalks. Join them together inside the first ring of petals. Make another six petals in the same way and attach them in the centre of the ring of petals.

 Roll a small ball of dough and flatten it slightly. Wet the back and gently press it in the centre of the circle of petals. Make some small holes in the centre of the flower using a cocktail stick.

 Make two small sunflowers as before, and arrange them either side of the first sunflower. The garland is now ready for baking. Bake at 120°C (250°F or Gas Mark ½) for about four hours.

Finishing the garland

 Once the garland has cooled, it is ready for painting.

- Dark green, for the large leaves
- While the dark green paint is still damp, mix a little red paint with water and brush it over the leaves
- Bright yellow mixed with a little brown to make the golden sunflower colour, for the petals
- Dark brown, for the centre of the sunflowers
- Golden dots, in the impressions made with the cocktail stick

When the paint is dry, apply a coat of varnish.

 Thread the wire through the holes at the top of the garland, twist the two ends to form a loop. Thread the ribbon through the front of the wire and tie a bow in it.

3
Sleeping
rabbits

The sleeping rabbits are a perfect
Valentine's Day present, but you
could easily change the message to
suit any occasion. Take your time
modelling the rabbit's faces, as
their expression sets the tone of
the piece. Much of the detail is
added when you paint the project,
creating a really impressive finish.
Actual size: length 126mm (5in),
height 90mm (3½in)

+ 3 tbs of h₂o
1 c flor
+ ¼ c of h₂o
½
c salt

DOUGHCRAFT

Salt dough
100g (4oz) plain flour *½ cup*
50g (2oz) table salt *¼ cup*
50ml (2fl oz or ¼ cup) water
You will need:
Small heart cutter
Small flower cutter
Small leaf cutter
Cocktail stick
Green, orange, lilac, brown, white and bright red paints
Varnish

1 Roll a rope of dough, 126mm (5in) long and about 25mm (1in) thick. Trim the edges and make some log-like indentations in the front and back with a knife. Place the log on a baking tray.

2 Roll a table tennis-size ball of dough for the body of the rabbits, wet the top centre of the log and join on the ball.

3 To make the rabbits' heads roll two balls the size of large marbles. Roll four tiny balls for the cheeks, flatten and join them at the front of the faces, leaving a small space between each cheek. Smooth out the edges of the cheeks with a damp paintbrush.

4 Make the whisker parts from two pea-size balls of dough. Cut these in half and roll four tiny balls from the four pieces. Flatten them between your finger and thumb. Join these in between the cheeks. Make tiny holes for the whiskers with a cocktail stick. Roll a tiny ball for each of the noses.

5 Roll four small ropes of dough approximately 13mm (½in) long. Flatten and curl them between your finger and thumb to form the ears.

6 Cut a tiny strip of dough to make a bow for the lefthand rabbit (see Making Bows on page 14).

Cut some decorative flowers and heart shapes from rolled-out dough using cutters. Make three carrots from small tapered ropes and join them to the log.

Bake the finished item at 120°C (250°F or Gas Mark ½) for about four hours.

Finishing the sleeping rabbits

Once the sleeping rabbits have been cooled completely, you can paint them.

- Green, for the leaf and carrot tops
- Orange, for the carrots
- Lilac, for the flower
- Yellow, for the other flower and bow
- Mix brown and white to make cream, for the soles of the rabbits' feet and the whisker parts
- Light brown, for the noses and the soles of the feet
- Bright red, for the blanket and hearts
- Black, for the rabbits' sleeping eyes and the valentine's message.

Finally, give the rabbits cheeks a little blusher with watery red paint. When the paint is dry apply two coats of varnish.

Wet the top of the body and join the finished heads. Roll out some dough and cut a 150 x 50mm (6 x 2in) rectangle. Wrap it around the rabbits to form a blanket, crossing the ends over at the front.

Roll four small balls of dough, flatten and squeeze them into oval feet shapes. Join the feet to the bottom of the blanket curling them outwards.

4
Basket of roses

Woven salt dough can create a
wonderful effect. This basket of
roses, made from salt dough, was
baked and varnished to give it a
warm yellow colour. The delicate
roses, leaves and buds are made
from bread dough. The lid is
separate from the rest of the
basket, concealing the oasis on
which the roses are arranged.
Actual size: 150mm (6in) long

Making the basket

Salt dough

225g (8oz) plain flour

100g (4oz) table salt

100ml (4fl oz or ½ cup) water

You will need:

Small oval baking dish, about 160mm (6½in) long and 120mm (4¾in) wide

Strip of strong cardboard measuring 410 x 50mm (16 x 2in)

Kitchen foil

460mm (½yd) ribbon

1 Roll out some dough until it is quite thin, and cut about 20 strips, 13mm (½in) wide. Weave the strips together (see Weaving Dough on page 15) to make a lid for the oval dish. Turn the dish upside down on the woven dough and cut around it.

2 Make a thin twist to fit around the edge of the lid (see Making Twists on page 16). Join the rope around the edge of the lid and trim off any excess dough.

  Measure the woven lid and cut it in half. Cut 25mm (1in) square from each of the four corners.

 Weave some more dough, enough to cover the inside of the dish. Lightly grease the inside of the dish and lay the woven dough inside. Trim around the edge of the dish. Make a twist and attach it to the edges of the woven basket.

 Make a thick twist for the handle and place it over the cardboard support, tucking the ends in between the cardboard and the inside of the dish.

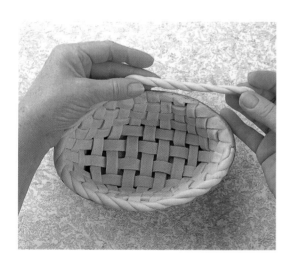

 Place the basket and lid on a baking tray and bake at 120°C (250°F or Gas Mark ½) for about four hours. Allow the basket to cool before removing the cardboard support. Apply two coats of varnish to the basket and lid, both inside and out.

 Glue the ends of the cardboard strip together to make a circle and cover it with kitchen foil. Place the foil-covered circle in the centre of the basket (this will support the handle while baking).

DOUGHCRAFT

Making the roses
Bread dough
50g (2oz) white bread without the crusts
½ tablespoon of white acrylic paint
1½ tablespoons of PVA glue
½ level teaspoon of glycerine or glycerol
You will need:
Small piece oasis
Florist's wire
32 cocktail sticks
Fast-setting glue
Pink and green paint

 Divide the dough into quarters. Colour three quarters pink for the roses and buds and one part green for the leaves (see Colouring Bread Dough on page 10). Wrap the colours separately in plastic wrap or cling film

 You will need to make 16 roses and 8 rose buds (see page 17 for details of how to make these). Glue each flower on to a cocktail stick using PVA glue. Stick the flowers in oasis to dry.

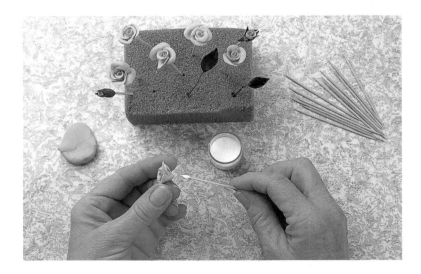

 Roll out the leftover green dough. Cut out eight leaves with the cutter. Make some leaf markings to one side of the leaves. Attach the leaves to the florist's wire by dabbing PVA glue on the back of the leaf and lay the wire against it. Stand these up in the oasis to dry.

 Apply two coats of varnish to the roses, buds and leaves and leave them to dry in the oasis.

Finishing the basket of roses

 Cut the oasis into chunks and put it in the basket. Don't over fill the basket, or the lid will not fit on top.

 Place the two halves of the lid on the basket. Put some fast-setting glue where the two halves meet and hold it in a slightly upward position for a few seconds until the glue has dried.

 Arrange the roses, buds and leaves around the edge of the basket, pushing the ends of the cocktail sticks and wires into the oasis. Cut the ribbon in half and tie bows around each end of the basket handle.

5
Three
ducks out
for a walk

These ducks are charming, cheerful
and easy to make. The body of
each duck is made from a ball of
dough, so you will need to make
sure that each model is baked for
long enough to ensure that the
dough is completely dry.
Actual size: large duck 75mm (3in),
medium duck 64mm (2½in), small
duck 50cm (2in)

Salt dough

170g (6oz) plain flour

75g (3oz) table salt

75ml (3fl oz or ⅓ cup) water

You will need:

Cocktail stick

25mm (1in) round cutter

White, blue, black and yellow paints

Varnish

Making the large duck

1 Roll some dough into a golf-size ball and gently press it down on a work surface to flatten the bottom.

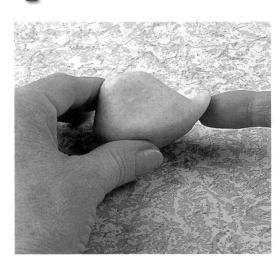

2 Pinch out one side of the ball into a tail shape with your finger and thumb.

3 Make the feet from two small flattened balls. Join the feet to the body. Make some markings on the top of the feet to make them look webbed.

4 Roll a table tennis-size ball of dough and join it to the body. Pinch the front of the head to form a beak. Make the eyes using the point of a cocktail stick.

5 To make the wings, roll two small balls of dough and flatten them between your finger and thumb. Pinch one end of each flattened ball out to form a wing. Join the wings to the body. Make some feather-like markings with a knife.

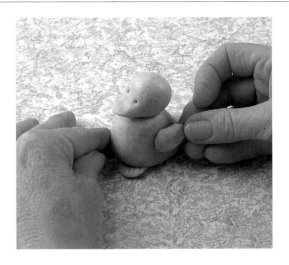

 Follow these instructions for the medium and small-size ducks. Make sure each duck is slightly smaller than the last.

 Roll out some dough until it is 3mm (⅛in) thick. Cut a 75mm (3in) square. Cut the square in half diagonally to make two triangles. Wrap one triangle around the duck, crossing over the two ends at the front. Roll a small ball for the button and join it to the front of the scarf.

 Place the ducks on a baking tray and bake them at 120°C (250°F or Gas Mark ½) for about four hours.

Finishing the ducks

 Using the other half of the triangle, cut out two circles for the hat with the round cutter. Wet the top of the head and join one circle to it. Cut a half moon shape from the other circle and join it to the front of the hat. Make a small pompom for the top of the hat.

 When the ducks are cool you can paint them.
- White, for the ducks body, front button, pompom, and the spots on the scarf and hat
- Blue, for the scarf and hat
- Yellow, for the beak and feet
- Black, for the eyes

When the paint is dry apply two coats of varnish.

6
Flowers
for a
friend

You may have a special friend who
would love to have something
personal made by you. This woven
basket is made from salt dough
and the flowers, leaves and corn
are made from delicately coloured
bread dough, arranged on a piece
of oasis tucked inside the basket.
Actual size: 190 x 100mm
(7½ x 4in)

Making the basket

Salt dough

225g (8oz) plain flour

100g (4oz) table salt

100ml (4fl oz or ½ cup) water

You will need:

Kitchen foil

230mm (9in) ribbon

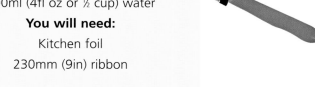

Roll out the salt dough until it is about 6mm (¼in) thick. Cut it into strips about 13mm (½in) wide and about 150mm (6in) long. Weave two pieces of dough measuring 90 x 125mm (3½ x 5in) and 90 x 75mm (3½ x 3in), (see Weaving Dough on page 15).

Lay the smaller piece of woven dough on the top of the larger piece with the bottom edges together.

Trim off the woven dough to make a perfect 'V' shape. Join the two pieces together to make the basket.

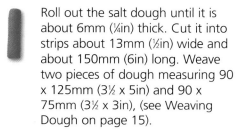
Carefully place the basket on a baking tray. Tuck some crumpled kitchen foil inside the front pocket to keep it open while it is baking.

Make a twisted handle 280mm (11in) long (see Making Twists on page 16) and join it to the basket at either side.

Bake the basket at 120°C (250°F or Gas Mark ½) for about three hours. When the container is cool, remove the foil. Varnish it, inside and out, and leave it to dry.

Making the flowers, leaves and corn
Bread dough

25g (1oz) white bread without the crusts

¼ level tablespoon white acrylic paint

¾ level tablespoon PVA glue

¼ level teaspoon glycerine or glycerol

You will need:

Small scissors

Small piece oasis

Florist's wire

Pink, green and cream paints

Divide the bread dough into four pieces and colour them pink, cream and green. Leave one piece white (see Colouring Bread Dough on page 10).

You will need to make the following (see pages 16 and 17 for details):

- twelve pink roses,
- twenty-four ears of corn, twelve green and twelve cream,
- eight cream leaves.

Attach each piece to florist's wire with PVA glue. To attach the leaves, dab some PVA glue on the back of the leaf and lay a length of florist's wire on the back so that the wire is lying flat against the leaf. Stand the finished shapes in oasis to dry.

Roll some very tiny balls of white dough and attach these to florist's wire with a dab of PVA glue. Use these small fantasy flowers to fill in any spaces when you arrange the flowers in the basket.

Varnish all the flowers, leaves and corn and leave to dry.

Finishing the basket

Cut a small piece of oasis and push it in the front pocket of the basket. Arrange the flowers, leaves and corn in the oasis.

Tie the ribbon around the basket handle in a bow. Take two lengths of florist's wire and twist them together. Push the wire through the back of the ribbon and twist it to form a hanging loop.

7
Scarecrow

The scarecrow is simple and fun to
make. His hair, and the straw
stuffing escaping from his cuffs and
shirt, are made by pushing salt
dough through a garlic press.
The legs and arms are tied with
twine to give the finished item a
rustic feel.
Actual size: height 126mm (5in)

DOUGHCRAFT

Salt dough
110g (4oz) plain flour
50g (2oz) table salt
50ml (2fl oz or ¼ cup) water

You will need:
Garlic press
Hairpin cut to 25mm (1in)
510mm (20in) parcel string
Cocktail stick
Scrap of fabric with a rough texture
Green, red, orange, light brown and black paints

 Roll two small finger-sized ropes of dough to make the legs. Cut them to 38mm (1½in) long. Join them together on the inside at one end with a little water. Make sure that the legs are apart at the bottom.

 Roll out some dough, about 13mm (½in) thick, and cut a rectangle, 25 x 38mm (1 x 1½in). Join the rectangle to the top of the legs. Make a vertical line down the front of the body for the shirt. Make some buttonholes with a cocktail stick.

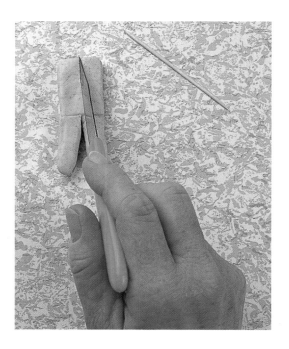

Roll out some dough to about 6mm (¼in) thick. Cut a rectangle 50 x 90mm (2 x 3½in). Press the dough against the textured cloth. Lay the piece in front of you with the 90mm (3½in) edges at the top and bottom. Mark the centre of the bottom edge lightly with a knife. This piece will make the trousers.

 Measure 25mm (1in) up from the mark you made on the bottom edge and cut the dough. Join the trouser legs. The trousers will be too long, but don't worry. Gather the top of the trousers around the waist and tie a piece of string as a belt, making a knot at the front. Tie pieces of string loosely around the ankles of the trousers.

DOUGHCRAFT

 Cut a 13mm (½in) square of thinly rolled out dough to make the patch, and join it to the trousers. Make some holes around the patch with the end of a cocktail stick.

 Roll a small finger-sized rope of dough about 64mm (2½in) long. Cut this length in half to make the arms. Join the arms to the body. Cut two lengths of string and wrap them around the wrists.

 To make the waistcoat roll out some dough about 6mm (¼in) thick and cut two 25 x 50mm (1 x 2in) rectangles. Press these two pieces on a scrap of fabric, then peel them off, leaving a textured pattern. Snip around the lower edges and the armholes and join the two pieces to the body.

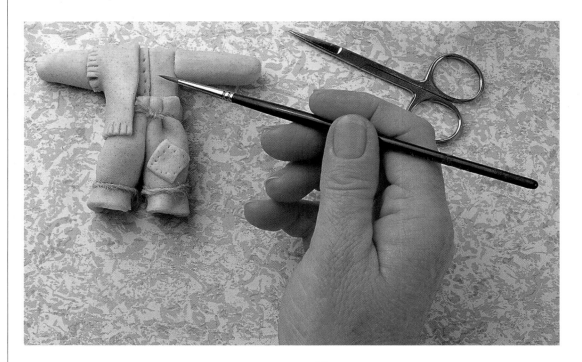

 Roll a large marble-size ball of dough for the head and join it to the body. Make the eyes and mouth with the end of a cocktail stick. Make a nose from a small triangle of dough.

Make the scarf from a thin rope of dough and join it around the neck, crossing it over at the front.

 Push some dough through the garlic press, and join some strands to the head around the face. Push some strands in the end of the arms, legs and inside the front of the scarecrow's body.

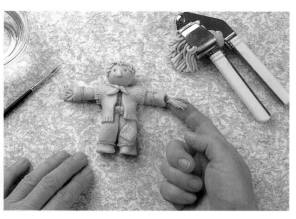

 Make the hat from two small balls of dough and join it to the head. Cut a small piece off the back of the hat so the scarecrow can lie flat. Push a hairpin in the back of the head and lay the scarecrow on a baking tray.

 Make the blackbird from a 25mm (1in) long cigar shape. Flatten one end to make the tail and make a snip on each side with scissors for the wings. Join the bird to the scarecrow's left arm.

 Bake at temperature 120°C (250°F or Gas Mark ½) for about four hours.

Finishing the scarecrow

 Once the scarecrow has cooled completely you can begin painting him.
- Green, for the shirt
- Red, for the scarf
- Watery orange, for the nose and patch
- Light brown, for the straw and hair
- Black, for the blackbird and mouth

Once the paint is dry, apply two or three coats of varnish.

8
Flower
ball in a
pot

Use your imagination to create all
kinds of flowers for this flower ball.
The finished item makes a perfect
table centrepiece or mantelpiece
decoration. The delicate flowers are
made from bread dough, which
was coloured before the modelling
process began. Details were
added with paint when the dough
was dry and a decorative double
bow was added as a final touch.

DOUGHCRAFT

Bread dough

50g (2oz) white bread without the crusts

½ level tablespoon white acrylic paint

1½ tablespoons PVA glue

½ level teaspoon of glycerine or glycerol

You will need:

Small terracotta plant pot

Small bag plaster of Paris

1 large finger-thick twig from the garden, 200mm (8in) long

1 small oasis ball

Garlic press

Small flower and leaf cutters

300mm (12in) ribbon

Five or six colours of paint including green

Making the flower ball

1 Push the twig about 38mm (1½in) into the centre of the oasis ball. Remove it, put some glue on the end and push it back into the same hole and leave it to dry.

2 Block the hole at the bottom of the plant pot with a little crushed newspaper, making sure nothing can leak out. Mix the plaster of Paris according to the instructions on the packet, and fill the plant pot up to about 25mm (1in) from the top.

3 Push the end of the twig into the centre of the plaster of Paris, and hold it steady for a minute until the twig can stand straight alone. Don't move the twig around or it will not dry straight. Leave the plaster to set.

4 Cut off one quarter of the dough and colour it green (see Colouring Bread Dough on page 10). Divide up the rest of the dough and colour it five or six different colours.

5 Push some green dough through a garlic press to make grass, and glue some so that it covers the top of the plaster of Paris inside the plant pot. Save any grass you have left over to fill in any small spaces between the flowers.

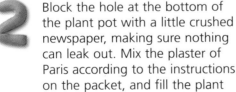

Roll out a some green dough so it is fairly thin, and cut out ten leaves with the cutter.

 Make seven more small flowers with the leftover coloured dough, and glue some to the grass at the top of the pot. Attach a few of the flowers so that they cascade down the front of the pot.

 When all the flowers are stuck on the pot you may wish add some detail with paint using contrasting colours.

Making the flowers

 Make about forty-five flowers using flower cutters (see Making Flowers on page 17). Glue all the flowers to the oasis ball using PVA glue. Glue the leaves between the flowers. Fill in any spaces between the flowers with grass and leaves.

Finishing
the flower ball in a pot

 Apply two coats of varnish to the flowers, grass and leaves. Wrap the ribbon around the twig, and tie it in a bow at the front. I used two different colours of ribbon to create a contrast.

9
Mother rabbit with babies

By the time that you have painted and varnished these adorable rabbits, you will find this project difficult to give away. Although it looks quite complicated, this project is simple to make. Read through the instructions carefully before you start, and follow each step in turn.
Actual size: height 150mm (6in)

DOUGHCRAFT

Salt dough

170g (6oz) plain flour

75g (3oz) table salt

75ml (3fl oz or ⅜cup) water

You will need:

2 small black plastic beads

Cocktail stick

Hairpin cut to 25mm (1in)

Kitchen foil

Mint green, white, black, light brown and strong pink paints

To make the legs, roll a finger-size rope 100mm (4in) long. Cut the rope in half, and lay the two halves on a baking tray. Round off the end of each leg to make the feet. Make indentations on the feet.

Make two small frills to fit around each ankle (see Making Frills on page 15). Join the two legs together at the top.

Roll a fat rope, about 30mm (1⅛in) thick. Flatten the rope slightly with the palm of your hand. Cut a piece measuring 50mm (2in) from the rope. Join the body to the legs.

Roll out some dough until it is fairly thin. Cut a rectangle measuring 50 x 150mm (2 x 6in). Gather the long edge of the rectangle in to about 56mm (2¼in). Flatten the gathered edge slightly with your finger, and trim off any excess dough to make a straight edge.

Lay the skirt on the body, so that the frills on the ankles just peep out of the bottom hem. Join the underside of the gathered edge to the waist, tucking the edges around the back of the body. Fold the two side edges of the skirt over in a small hem. Crush some small pieces of kitchen foil, and push them under the skirt to stop it from going flat when baked.

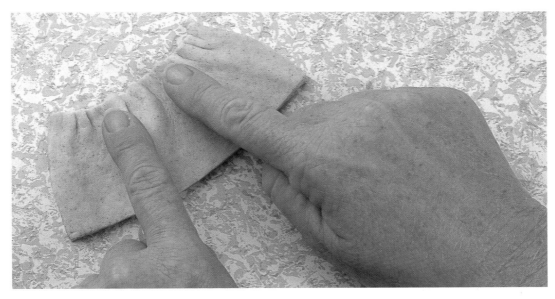

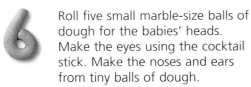

Roll five small marble-size balls of dough for the babies' heads. Make the eyes using the cocktail stick. Make the noses and ears from tiny balls of dough.

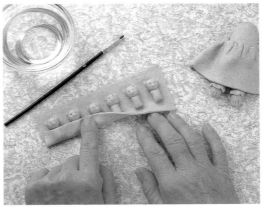

Roll a small finger-size rope of dough 64mm (2½in) long. Cut the rope into five pieces each measuring 13mm (½in) and join a baby's head to one end.

To make the apron, roll out some dough until it is quite thin. Cut a rectangle measuring 64 x 150mm (2½ x 6in). Wet the back of each baby rabbit, and lay them in a line on the apron, 20mm (¾in) from the bottom edge.

Wet the bottom edge of the apron and turn 20mm (¾in) up from the bottom edge. Gently press the material between each baby rabbit making sure that the edges of the apron are sealed. Gather the top of the apron in to 56mm (2¼in) Join the apron to the dress. Make a waistband from a thin strip, and join it to the top of the apron.

 Make the arms from a small finger rope of dough 100mm (4in) long. Cut this in half and round off one end of each arm. Make three marks at the rounded ends.

 Roll out some dough and cut two pieces measuring 38 x 75mm x (1½ x 3in). Wet the arms and place the sleeves over them and gather them in at the shoulders and wrists, tucking the edges around the back. Join the arms to the side of the body. Join each paw to the sides of the apron.

 Make the head from a golf-size ball of dough. Join the head to the body. Roll two tiny ropes of dough for the cheeks and join them to the head, leaving a small gap in the centre for the whisker parts. Smooth the cheeks with a paintbrush.

 To make the whisker parts, roll two pea-size balls of dough, flatten and join them between the cheeks. Make some small holes in these with the point of a cocktail stick. Make a nose from a small triangle of dough.

 Bake the finished model at 100°C (200°F or Gas Mark ¼) for about five hours.

Finishing the mother rabbit with babies

Once the mother rabbit has cooled, you can paint it.

- Mint green, for the dress and bonnet (not the frill)
- White, for the ankle frills, apron and the frills around the bonnet
- Black, for babies' eyes, and around the mother's eyes
- Light brown, for the whiskers
- Strong pink, for the mother's and babies' noses and ears. Use the same pink to paint small dots on the mother's dress
- Water down the pink, and give the mother's cheeks some colour

Apply two coats of varnish.

14 Mark out two small circle shapes for the eyes with a knife. Push the knife in a little further all the way around the circle and lift off the top surface of the dough. Wet each eyehole and press a bead into each of the holes.

15 Roll out some dough until it is quite thin. Cut a piece measuring 20 x 90mm (¾ x 3½in) to make the bonnet. Make a frill to fit around the inside edge of the bonnet and join it around the head. Then join the bonnet over the frill.

16 Make some ears by rolling two thin ropes of dough 20mm (¾in) long. Flatten and taper one end of each rope. Make a small vertical line on each of the ears using a knife. Join the ears to the top of the bonnet. Push the hairpin in the top centre of the hat towards the back.

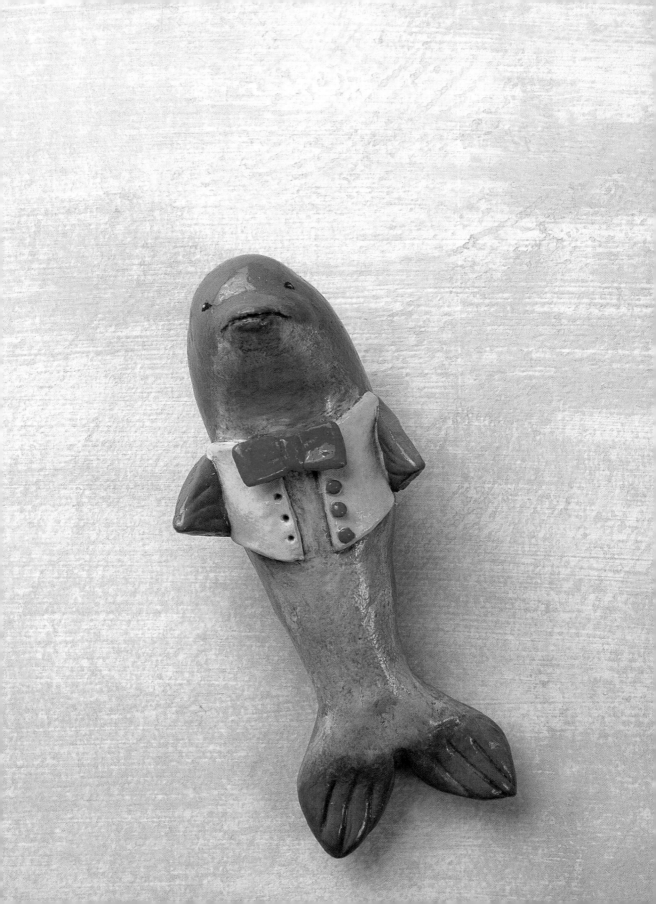

10
Dolphin

Someone you know will love this
dolphin. By adapting this simple
shape, you can make a set of
leaping dolphins for a wall or
mobile. The dolphin itself is simply
shaped from salt dough, with fins
and a waistcoat added.
Much of the detail is added at
painting stage.
Actual size: 150mm (6in) long.

DOUGHCRAFT

Salt dough

50g (2oz) plain flour

25g (1oz) table salt

25ml (1fl oz or ⅛cup) water

Break or cut off a walnut size piece of dough from the allowance,

and wrap it in plastic wrap or cling film.

You will need:

Hairpin cut to 25mm (1in)

Cocktail stick

Light grey, black, yellow and blue paints

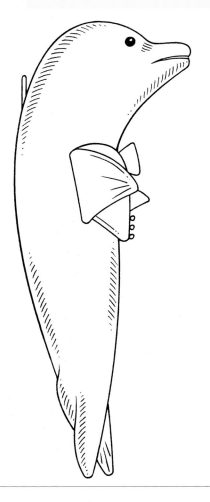

1 Roll a fat rope 150mm (6in) long. Squeeze the rope about 25mm (1in) from one end with your finger and thumb to make the tail.

2 Flatten the tail and make a 13mm (½in) slit in the middle. Pinch each side of the tail into a slight point and score some lines on each side of the tail with the knife.

3 Smooth and slightly bend the opposite end of the rope to make the head. Roll a small marble-size ball for the beak and join it to the face.

4 Shape the beak and smooth out the edges with a damp paint-brush. Make a small slit around the beak with the knife.

5 Roll out the rest of the dough until it is quite thin. To make the waistcoat, cut two strips, 13 x 38mm (½ x 1½in). Cut the ends of the strips diagonally.

Join the strips to the dolphin's body, leaving a 6mm (¼in) in between them at the front. Make three buttonholes with the cocktail stick and make three buttons for the other side.

 Cut a 13mm (½in) strip for a bow tie. To make the fins, cut two 20mm (¾ x ¾in) squares. Cut a triangle from each of these squares with the knife. Join the fins to the dolphin.

 Push the hairpin in the back of the dolphin's head. Put the dolphin on a baking sheet and bake at 120°C (250°F or Gas Mark ½) for about four hours.

Finishing the dolphin

 Once the dolphin has cooled, you can paint him.
- Light grey, for the body of the dolphin
- Add some white paint to the grey, for the front of the body
- Black, for the lips and the eyes
- Bright yellow, for the waistcoat
- Blue, for the bow tie and buttons.

After the paint is dry, apply two coats of varnish.

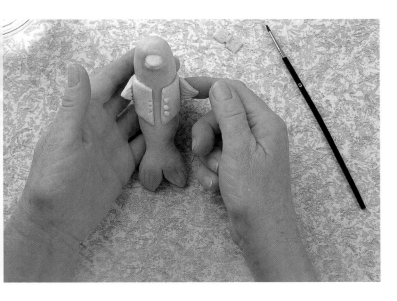

11
Tractor

You can hang this colourful tractor
up anywhere in the home. It would
make an ideal gift for any child.
You can change the animals in
the trailer if you want, perhaps
using the favourites of the person
you have in mind.
Actual size: length 150mm (6in),
height 75mm (3in)

Salt dough
100g (4oz) plain flour
50g (2oz) table salt
50ml (2fl oz or ¼ cup) water

You will need:
2 cocktail sticks
2 hairpins cut to 25mm (1in)
Garlic press
Kitchen foil
25mm (1in) round cutter
38mm (1½in) round cutter
Brightly coloured paints

Making the tractor

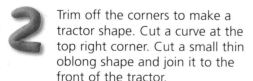

1 Roll out the dough until it is about 13mm (½in) thick. Cut a rectangle measuring 38 x 90mm (1½ x 3½in). Cut off a small step to make the driver's seat.

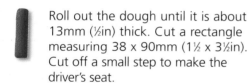

2 Trim off the corners to make a tractor shape. Cut a curve at the top right corner. Cut a small thin oblong shape and join it to the front of the tractor.

3 Cut out two tractor wheels using the large and small cutters from the rolled out dough. Make some small cuts with a knife on the sides of the wheels. Roll two small balls of dough, flatten them and join them to the centre of the wheels. Roll five tiny balls to make the wheel nuts.

4 Roll out some more dough and cut a rectangle measuring 38 x 64mm (1½ x 2½in) to make the trailer. Roll a 6mm (¼in) strip of dough and join it to the top of the trailer.

5 Roll out some dough so that it is 6mm (¼in) thick and cut out two wheels for the trailer using the small round cutter. Roll two small balls, flatten them and join them to the centre of the wheels. Make a hole in the centre of the flattened small balls with a cocktail stick.

Roll a small marble-size ball of dough and push a cocktail stick through it. Push one end of the cocktail stick into the back of the tractor, and the other end into the front of the trailer. Push the tractor and trailer firmly together.

 Attach the wheels to the tractor and trailer. Tuck some crushed kitchen foil under the bottom of the wheels to prop them up.

Making the driver, pig and sheep

 To make the driver, roll a finger-size rope about 20mm (¾in) long, a small marble-size ball for the head and a small ball for the hat. Make the pompom out of a tiny ball of dough and add it to the top of the hat. Make a driving wheel from a small flattened ball and join it to the tractor in front of the driver. Make a small arm and join it to the body and the driving wheel.

 To make the pig, roll a small marble-size ball. Roll a small ball for the nose. Make holes for the eyes and nostrils with a cocktail stick. Make the ears from two very tiny pieces of flattened dough.

 To make the sheep, roll a small ball for the head. Make the eyes and nose with the end of a cocktail stick. Push some dough through a garlic press for the sheep's wool.

 Roll two thin ropes to make the funnel. Join the funnel to the tractor.

 Push the hairpins in both ends of the tractor and trailer and place it on a baking tray. Bake at 120°C (250°F or Gas Mark ½) for about four hours.

Finishing the tractor

 I used bright primary colours to give the tractor a cheerful feel. Apply two coats of varnish when the paint is dry.

12
Country
plant pot

Any plant would look attractive in
this pot. The country scene design
is very simple and could be adapted
to suit a large or small pot as
required. The scene itself is made
from coloured bread dough.

DOUGHCRAFT

Bread dough

50g (2oz) white bread without the crusts

½ tablespoon of white acrylic paint

1½ level tablespoons of PVA glue

½ level teaspoon glycerine or glycerol

You will need:

1 medium-size terracotta garden plant pot (not plastic)

Cocktail stick

Small blossom cutter

Small amount of pale yellow matt finish emulsion paint

Small piece of sponge

Sky blue, dark green, dark brown and white paints

1 Divide the bread dough in half. Colour one half dark brown. Divide the other half into two pieces and colour one piece dark green. Leave the remaining piece white. Wrap each piece in plastic wrap or cling film.

2 Make sure the pot is clean and dry. Paint the pot, inside and out, with the yellow paint. When this is dry paint the top edge of the pot with sky blue paint and leave the pot to dry.

3 Sponge paint the bottom of the pot with dark green water-based paint. Dip the sponge into the paint, then, starting at the bottom of the pot, dab the paint on the pot until about three quarters of the pot is covered.

4 Paint some white clouds over the blue sky around the top edge of the plant pot.

5 Before you begin making the bread dough shapes, mark the position of the pieces on the pot with a pencil. Stick the pieces on the pot with PVA glue as soon as you have made them, so that they don't dry out. Leave the plant pot to dry for eight hours.

Finishing the pot

6 Add final touches of paint with a fine paintbrush. Once the paint is dry, apply two coats of acrylic varnish.

COUNTRY PLANT POT

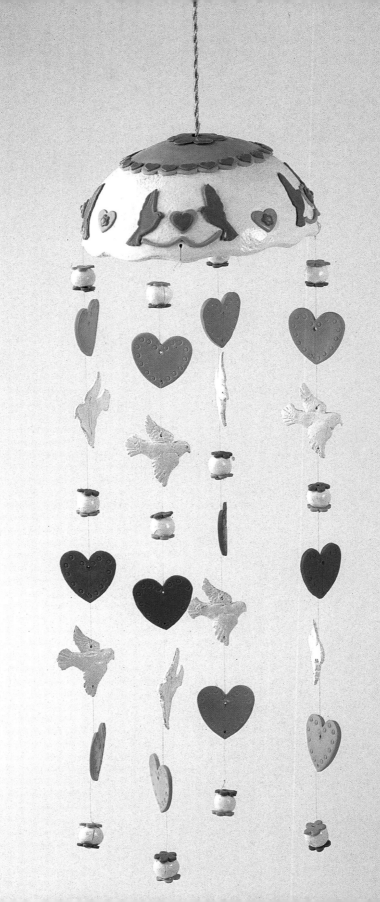

13
Heart
and dove
mobile

This delicate mobile will attract
attention in any home. The hearts
and doves create a tranquil
atmosphere. The top part of the
mobile is made from salt dough,
while the hanging decorations,
the hearts and doves, are made
from bread dough.
Actual size: 460mm (18in) high

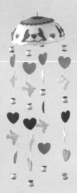

DOUGHCRAFT

Salt dough
100g (4oz) plain flour
50g (2oz) table salt
50ml (2fl oz or ¼ cup) water

Bread dough
50g (2oz) white bread without crusts
½ level tablespoon of white acrylic paint
1½ tablespoons PVA glue
½ teaspoon glycerine or glycerol

You will need:
2 metres (approximately 2 yards) thin transparent fishing wire
Large and small drinking straws
Small round fruit or soup bowl, approximately 100mm (4in) diameter
Pea-size bead (plastic or wood)
Outer cover of a ballpoint pen
Length of thin cord measuring 300mm (12in)
15 cocktail sticks
Medium-size, small and tiny blossom flower cutters
Medium-size dove cutter
Small bird cutter
Large, small and tiny heart cutters
Large round fluted pastry cutter, approximately 75mm (3in) diameter
Small ring (brass or plastic)
Small piece of oasis
Blue and pink paints

Making the mobile top

Divide the bread dough into thirds and colour one piece pink, one blue, and leave the remaining piece white. Wrap the coloured dough up separately in plastic wrap or cling film.

Lightly grease the inside of the small bowl. Roll out the salt dough so that it is 6mm (¼in) thick. Lay the dough inside the bowl and trim off the edges using the knife. Make a hole with the large hole drinking straw in the centre of the dough.

Make four holes around the inside edge of the bowl edge using the small hole drinking straw, spacing them out evenly.

Place the bowl on a baking tray, and bake it at 120°C (250°F or Gas Mark ½) for about two hours. Remove the dough from the bowl and allow it cool. If you find that underside of the dough isn't quite dry, turn it upside down on the baking tray and return it to the oven for further baking.

Hang up the top of the mobile using the cord and bead, it will make it easier to paint and decorate. Paint the bowl shape white inside and out. Leave it to dry, then varnish it.

Decorating the mobile top

 Roll out some pink bread dough until it is quite thin and cut a circle using the large round fluted cutter. Roll out some blue bread dough and cut a flower shape using the medium-sized blossom cutter. Put some glue on one side of the blue flower and join it to it to the centre of the pink fluted circle. Make a hole in the centre of the daisy and fluted circle with the large hole drinking straw.

 Put some PVA glue on the underside of the fluted circle, and thread it over the end of the cord and bring it down to join the top of the bowl shape. Cut out some tiny hearts and glue them around the edge of the pink fluted circle.

 The edges of the mobile are decorated with shapes cut from thinly rolled bread dough. You will need to cut:
- 8 medium-size pink hearts
- 8 medium-size doves
- 4 small hearts
- 4 small pink blossoms
- 4 small blue blossoms
- 4 tiny pink balls and 4 tiny blue balls to finish the blossoms
- 4 tiny pink ropes to join the doves together.

Arrange the shapes as shown.

To make the mobile shapes

 Using the large heart cutter cut out eight pink hearts and four blue. Make a hole at the top and bottom of each heart using the small hole drinking straw. Make some indentations around the outside edges of the hearts using the pen cover.

To make the beads, cut twelve pink flowers and twelve blue with the tiny flower cutter. Roll twelve small marble-size balls of white dough. Slide the ball to the centre of a cocktail stick. Add a pink and blue flower to either side of the bead. Push the point of the cocktail stick into the piece of oasis. Make another 11 flower beads.

Using the dove cutter, cut out eight doves. Make a hole at the top and bottom of each dove using the small hole drinking straw.

Leave all the bread dough parts to dry, then varnish them on both sides.

Assembling the mobile

Cut the fishing wire into four equal lengths, and tie them to the holes in the top of the mobile.

Each of the mobile shapes needs to be threaded in order, leaving 25mm (1in) between each piece. Tie a knot under each flower bead to keep it in place. The order from the top of the thread should be: flower bead, pink heart, dove, flower bead, blue heart, dove, pink heart, flower bead. Knot the end of each string firmly.

14
Parachute
Man

This parachute man would look
great hanging from a ceiling in a
playroom or nursery. The parachute
is made from salt dough which is
baked into a curve.
Actual size: 460mm (18in) high
including cord

DOUGHCRAFT

Salt dough

225g (8oz) plain flour

100g (4oz) table salt

100ml (4fl oz or ½ cup) water

You will need:

2 metres (approximately 2 yards) thin cord

32mm (1¼in) round cutter

50mm (2in) round cutter

Saucepan, which can go in the oven

4 cocktail sticks

Small hole drinking straw

Garlic press

Fast-setting glue

1 small ring (brass or plastic)

A variety of shades of paint for decoration

Making the parachute

 Roll ten finger ropes of dough 100mm (4in) long and trim the ends. Join the ropes together. Make a hole in the four corners of the finished parachute, 6mm (¼in) from the edges with the drinking straw.

Lay the saucepan on its side resting on the handle on a baking tray. Lightly grease the top of the saucepan. Lay the joined ropes on the curved edge of the pan. Bake at temperature 110°C (220°F or Gas Mark ¼) for about four and a half hours.

Making the parachute man

To make the legs, cut a piece of dough measuring 38 x 50mm (1½ x 2in). Cut a 25mm (1in) slit up the centre with a knife, to divide the legs. Cut a cocktail stick in half, and push one half up each of the legs from the bottom leaving 6mm (¼in) of the stick protruding.

Roll two small ropes of dough for the shoes. Make a small slit at the top of each shoe and holes either side of the slits with a cocktail stick. Join the shoes to the legs spearing them on the cocktail stick.

Stand the bottom half of the man up on his feet and smooth out the sides and back of the legs using a damp paintbrush.

To make the body, cut a piece of thick dough measuring 32 x 38mm (1¼ x 1½in) Make a vertical slit down the centre of the body to make a shirt. Make some buttonholes one side of the shirt using the point of a cocktail stick.

Cut off a quarter off the length of a cocktail stick. Push the longer piece through the centre body. Join the body to the top of the trousers.

Roll a thin strip of dough for the belt and buckle and join them around the waist.

Roll out some dough until it is 3mm (⅛in) thick. Cut a two pieces measuring 38 x 50mm (1½ x 2in). Lay both pieces in front of you and shape the armholes by cutting off the two top corners. Join one piece to the back of the body.

Cut the second piece in half. Join the pieces to the front of the body to make the jacket. Wet the side seams of the jacket and gently press them together. Smooth the seams with a damp paintbrush. Turn up the lower edge of the jacket with your finger and thumb.

Roll two finger ropes of dough, each measuring 45mm (1¾in) long for the arms. Flatten one end of each rope to make the hands and shape the fingers with a knife.

Cut two pieces of thin dough measuring 25 x 45mm (1 x 1¾in) to make the sleeves. Wet one side of each piece and wrap them around the arms. Join the arms to the body. Smooth the seams with a damp paintbrush. Turn the fingers inwards towards the body.

Make buttonholes on one side of the jacket with a cocktail stick. Stand the man up on his feet on the baking tray, supporting his arms with two coffee mugs turned upside-down.

Roll a large marble-size ball of dough for the head. Roll three pea-size balls of dough, one for the nose and two for the cheeks. Smooth the edges of the cheeks using a damp paintbrush. Make his eyes and mouth with the point of a cocktail stick. Join the head to the body.

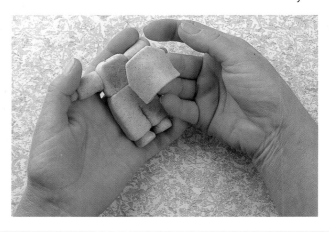

 Make a small scarf from a strip of thinly rolled out dough. Push a small amount of dough through the garlic press. Join the strands of dough to the top of the head.

 Cut a piece of thin dough measuring 13 x 75mm (½ x 3in). Join the piece to the head with the seam to the back. Cut a 32mm (1¼in) circle and join it to the back of the hat. Make the brim from a 50mm (2in) circle with the cutter. Cut another 32mm (1¼in) circle in the centre of the larger circle. Join the brim of the hat to the head. Smooth the seam with a damp paintbrush.

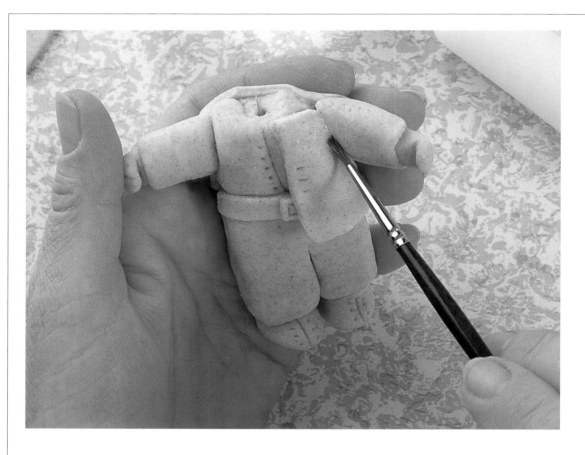

 Bake at temperature 120°C (250°F or Gas Mark ½) for about five hours.

Finishing and assembling the parachute man

 Paint the parachute man before you begin assembling him. I chose soft pastel tones and used a watery red to brighten up his cheeks and lips. Apply two coats of varnish when the paint is dry.

Fold the long piece of cord in half. Tie the ring in the centre of the two lengths with a few knots. Lay the four cords in front of you with the ring at the top.

 Thread the four ends of the cord through the four holes of the parachute so that the parachute is 230mm (9in) from the top of the ring.

 Keeping the cords level, tie a knot in the four corners to hold the parachute up. If you hang the parachute up somewhere, it will make it easier for you to join the man to the parachute and obtain the correct balance.

 Bring the two front cords down and wrap one end around and under his arms looping the two cords around his back. Tie these together in a knot. Bring the two cords down level, and tie them to cords at the back of the man. Put some fast-drying glue between the cord and the hands to secure it.

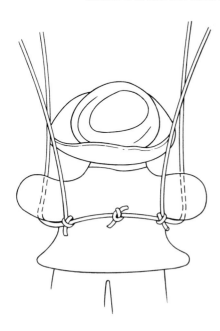

15
Sun and bumble bee mobile

This mobile is easy and fun to make. The bright colours and distinctive shapes will delight children and adults alike.

DOUGHCRAFT

Salt dough

225g (8oz) plain flour

100g (4oz) table salt

100ml (4fl oz or ½ cup) water

You will need:

1 small ring (brass or plastic)

1.5 metres (approximately 1½ yards) thin transparent fishing wire

4 strong hairpins

Fast-setting glue

1 small bead (plastic or wood)

300mm (12in) thin cord

Medium-size leaf cutter

Small round fruit or soup bowl, approximately 100mm (4in) diameter

Round fluted cutter 75mm (3in)

4 cocktail sticks

Small hole drinking straw

A range of brightly coloured paints

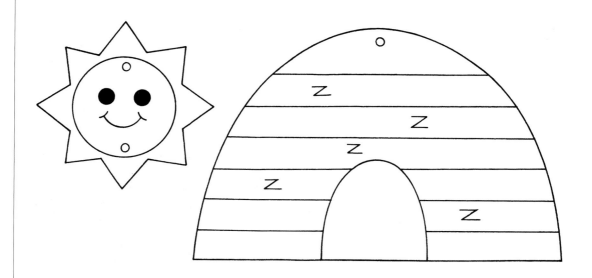

Making the bumble bee, hive and suns

1 Make a copy of the hive and sun templates on scrap paper. Cut out the hive and four suns from dough using the templates. Make a hole at the top centre of the hive and top and bottom of the suns with the drinking straw.

2 Cut eight straight pieces from the hairpins measuring 13mm (½in) long using the wire cutters. Trim the four rounded pieces to measure 13mm (½in) and pinch them together with the wire cutters to form an eyelet hole.

3 You will need to make four bumble bees. Each bumble bee has a head, a central section and a long tail. These three shapes are connected together on a cocktail stick. Make sure that no cocktail stick shows at either end of the bumble bee. Push two straight pieces of the hairpins 6mm (¼in) into the head to make the antennae. Roll two tiny balls of dough and push them onto the end of the antennae. Push the wire eyelet into the top of the body.

 To make the wings, roll out some dough and cut out two leaves using the cutter. Trim one end of each leaf with a knife to make a flat edge. Wet either side of the body and join the wings.

Making the top of the mobile

 Roll out some dough until it is 6mm (¼in) thick to coat the inside of the bowl, trim the edges. Make a hole in the centre of the bowl shape with the drinking straw. Make four holes around the inside edge of the bowl, 6mm (¼in) up from the top edge.

 Place the bowl, bees, hive and suns on a baking tray and bake at 110ºC (220ºF or Gas Mark ¼) for about four hours. If the bees' wings droop, prop them up with kitchen foil.

 Once baked, remove the dough from the bowl, placing it upside down on the baking tray and allow it to cool. The dough will not be fully baked on the outside, so that the fluted circle and flowers can be joined to it.

Decorating the top of the mobile

 Cut out a circle with the fluted cutter from thinly rolled dough. Make a hole in the centre of the circle with the large hole drinking straw. Wet one side of the circle and join it to the top of the mobile.

 Cut twenty leaves from thinly rolled dough and arrange them in a circle to form a flower on the bowl, between the holes. Make the centre of the flower from a small flattened ball and join it to the rest of the flower. Make three more flowers in the same way.

Return the top of the mobile to the oven and bake at 120°C (250°F or Gas Mark ½) for one hour.

Finishing and assembling the mobile

 Once the mobile, suns, hive and bumble bees have cooled, you can paint them. I used bright, cheerful colours. Apply two coats of varnish once the paint is dry.

 Put a drop of fast-setting glue in the eyelet holes of the bumble bees to keep the pins securely in place.

 Thread the bead on one end of the cord and secure with a knot. Thread the other end of the cord through the centre hole of the bowl and tie the ring to the end. If you hang the bowl up somewhere, it will make the mobile easier to assemble.

 Cut a length of fishing wire measuring 180mm (7in). Thread one end through the hole in the hive, and tie a few knots to secure it. Thread the other end of the same wire through the bead at the top and secure with a few knots.

 Cut the remaining wire into four pieces, and tie one length to each of the four holes around the top. Thread the four suns onto the wires (top hole first), and slide them up to within 75mm (3in) from the top of the mobile. Thread the other ends of the same wires through the four eyelet holes in the centre of the bees and tie them with a few knots.

16
Christmas table napkin rings

If you want to have something
original on your Christmas table,
then these napkin rings
will do the trick.
The quantities shown will
make six rings.

DOUGHCRAFT

Salt dough

100g (4oz) plain flour

50g (2oz) table salt

50ml (2fl oz or ¼ cup) water

You will need:

Outer cover of ballpoint pen

Cardboard tube, such as those inside kitchen paper

Cocktail stick

Kitchen foil

Red, green, gold and white paints

Making the napkin rings

Cut the cardboard tube into six equal pieces. Cover each piece, inside and out, with the kitchen foil.

Roll out some dough until it is quite thin. Cut six strips 38mm (1½in) wide and long enough to wrap around the tube.

Wrap one strip around each of the tubes, and join the ends of the strip together using a little water. Place the rolls so that the seams are at the bottom.

Make some indentations all the way around the edges with the ballpoint pen cover. Place the tubes on a baking tray.

Making Santa Claus

Roll a small finger rope of dough about 350mm (12in) long. Cut twelve arms each measuring 25mm (1in) long. Gently squeeze the end of each arm between your finger and thumb to make a hand. Make indentations for fingers with the knife.

Wet the underside of the arms, and join them to the top of the rings, leaving a 13mm (½in) space between the top of each arm.

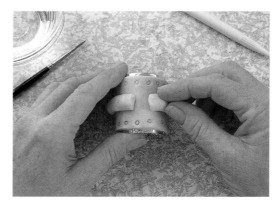

To make the head, roll a small marble-size ball of dough, and a tiny ball for the nose. Make holes for the eyes using the cocktail stick.

Make the beard by rolling a short thin rope of dough. Join the beard to the head. Make a hole in the centre of the beard for the mouth and rough up the surface to make it look fluffy.

Roll a small ball of dough to make the hat. Pinch and slightly roll one end. Put your finger in at the opposite end making a well and pull out the edge. Fold over the narrow end and secure with a little water. Wet the top of the head and join on the hat.

Roll a very thin rope for the edge of the hat. Rough up the rope with a cocktail stick to make it fluffy. Make a small pompom for the end of the hat. Repeat the process for the other five Santas. Stick the Santas' heads on to the napkin rings.

Bake the finished napkin rings at 120°C (250°F Gas Mark ½) for about two and a half hours.

Finishing the napkin rings

Once the rings are dry, you can paint them in festive colours.
- Dark green, for the outside of the rings
- Gold, for the markings on the edges of the rings
- Red, for the insides of the rings and the Santas' sleeves and hats
- White, for the beards. eyebrows, fur trimmings, pompoms and cuffs
- Watery red, for the noses.

Apply two coats of varnish when the paint is dry.

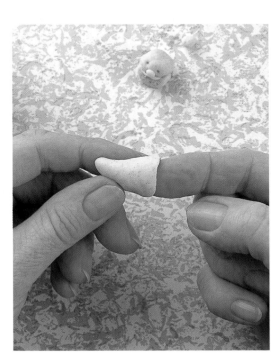

17
Christmas table name place

These Santa table name places are simple to make and complement the napkins rings described in the previous project.

DOUGHCRAFT

Salt dough

100g (4oz) plain flour

50g (2oz) table salt

50ml (2fl oz or ¼ cup) water

You will need:

Cocktail stick

Red, white, black and dark green paints

1 Roll a small finger rope of dough 75mm (3in) long. Cut the rope in half and shape the feet. Join the inside of the ropes together to make the legs.

2 To make the body, roll a large marble-size ball of dough. Wet the top end of the legs and join it to the body.

3 To make the arms and hands, roll a finger rope of dough 50mm (2in) long. Cut it in half and round off one end of each piece for the hands.

4 Roll a thin rope and cut it in half to make the cuffs. Wet either side of the body and top of the trousers and join the arms so that the hands rest on the legs.

5 Roll a large marble-size ball for the head. Make a nose from a tiny ball of dough. Make the eyes using the point of a cocktail stick. Join the head to the body.

6 To make a hat, roll a large marble-size ball of dough. Pinch the end. Put your finger into the opposite end of the ball making a well, and pull out the edge.

7 Make a beard and moustache from a thin rope of dough and join them to the face. Make a hole for the mouth between the moustache and beard with the point of the cocktail stick. Rough up the surface of the beard and moustache with the end of the knife or cocktail stick to make them look fluffy.

Join on the hat to the head. Fold over the narrow end of the hat, and secure with a little water. Roll a thin rope of dough and join it to the edge of the hat with the seam at the back. Rough up the surface of the rope around the edge of the hat with the point of a knife or cocktail stick.

 Make a pompom from a small ball and join it to the end of the hat. Then make five more table name places in the same way

 Place the Santas on a baking tray, and bake at 120°C (250°F or Gas Mark ½) for about three hours.

Finishing the name places

 Once the Santas are dry you can paint them. I used the same colour scheme as for the napkin rings, so that they complement each other.
- Red, for the Santas' suits
- Dark green, for the hands
- Black, for the boots and eye holes
- White, for the fur trimmings and the eyebrows
- Watery red, for their noses and cheeks

 Apply two coats of varnish. Cut some card into small pieces and write the names of your guests.

18 Christmas table centre-piece

What could be more attractive on a festive table than this delightful table centrepiece. You can guarantee to be the envy of all your friends.

Bread dough

50g (2oz) white bread without the crusts

½ level tablespoon white acrylic paint

1½ level tablespoons PVA glue

½ teaspoon of glycerine or glycerol

You will need:

Small primrose cutter

Small ivy leaf cutter

Holly cutter

Small, medium and large leaf cutters

Small black and yellow stamens

Florist's wire

Tweezers

150mm (6in) round gold cake board

Candle

280mm (11in) Ribbon

3 Petit four cases

Modelling tool

Small block oasis

Preparation

Divide the dough into five pieces and colour them as follows: one piece red, one piece pale yellow, one piece dark green, one piece light green and the remaining dough white. Take a tiny piece from the remaining white dough and colour it yellow or gold.

Cut about 40 or so pieces of florist's wire 50mm (2in) long.

Making the base

Cut a 50mm (2in) square and 25mm (1in) thick piece of oasis. Put the remaining oasis to one side, and use this to support the ivy, primroses, poinsettias, holly and berries when they are drying.

Glue the square of oasis onto the cakeboard, so that it is slightly off-centre about 32mm (1¼in) from the edge of the board. Leave it to dry. Glue the candle into the centre of the oasis.

Making Christmas roses

Roll a pea-size ball of white dough and flatten it to make the base of the flower.

To make a petal, roll a pea-size ball of dough and press it between your finger and thumb to make it very thin. Place the petal in the palm of your hand and roll the modelling tool from side to side on the dough to shape the petal into a cup. Put some glue on the base, and join the petal at the bottom.

Make another petal in the same way and join it to the first petal so that it overlaps. Put some glue between the edges of the petals to secure them. Make three more petals as before, joining them to the base and overlap them at the edges. Place the rose in a petit four case.

Roll a small ball of dough, and glue it to the centre of the rose. Cut ten yellow stamens to about 6mm (¼in) and push the ends into the centre ball using the tweezers.

Make two more roses and leave them to dry in the petit four cases.

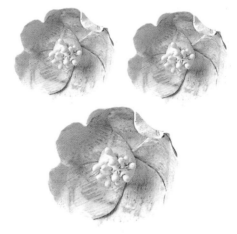

DOUGHCRAFT

Making ivy

Roll out some white dough and cut twelve ivy leaves using the cutter. Attach the leaves to wire by dabbing glue on one side of the leaf and pressing the wire halfway up the leaf. Stand the leaves up to dry in oasis.

Making the holly

Roll out some green dough and cut eight holly leaves using the cutter. Mark the leaf vein on one side of the leaf. Attach the leaves to wire and stand them in oasis, just as you did with the ivy leaves.

Making holly berries

Roll fourteen tiny balls of red dough and join them to the ends of the wires with some glue. Cut fourteen black stamens very short and push the end of each stamen into the centre of a berry using the tweezers. Stand the berries in oasis to dry.

Making poinsettias

 Roll a pea-size ball of dough and flatten it on a work surface. This piece will form the basis of the poinsettia.

 Roll out some red dough and cut out six leaves with the medium-size leaf cutter. Glue the six petals together to form a circle, so that they overlap at the edges. Put some glue on one side of the base, and join the circle of leaves.

 Roll out some more red dough, and cut out four leaves with the small leaf cutter. Put some glue in the centre of the first circle of leaves, and join the four small leaves to the centre.

 Roll seven tiny balls from yellow or gold dough. Put some glue in the centre of the flower and join the tiny balls.

 Using the light green dough, roll a small marble-size ball, and glue it at the bottom underneath the base. Roll out some more light green dough, and cut out three leaves using the large leaf cutter.

Make some leaf markings on one side of each leaf using the knife. Put some glue underneath the poinsettia flower and join the three leaves.

Dip the end of a wire into some glue, and push it 13mm (½in) into the bottom centre of the ball at the base of the poinsettia. Push the other end of the wire into the oasis, standing the flower up to dry. Make two more poinsettias.

Making primroses

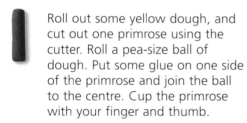

Roll out some yellow dough, and cut out one primrose using the cutter. Roll a pea-size ball of dough. Put some glue on one side of the primrose and join the ball to the centre. Cup the primrose with your finger and thumb.

Dip the end of a wire into some glue and push it into the centre of the ball. Cut four yellow stamens to 6mm (¼in) and push them into the centre of the primrose using the tweezers.

Push the other end of the wire into the oasis, standing the primrose up to dry. Make three more primroses.

Finishing and assembling the Christmas table centrepiece

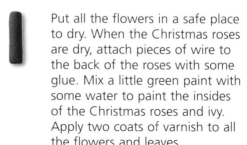

Put all the flowers in a safe place to dry. When the Christmas roses are dry, attach pieces of wire to the back of the roses with some glue. Mix a little green paint with some water to paint the insides of the Christmas roses and ivy. Apply two coats of varnish to all the flowers and leaves.

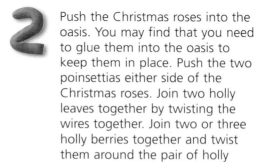

Push the Christmas roses into the oasis. You may find that you need to glue them into the oasis to keep them in place. Push the two poinsettias either side of the Christmas roses. Join two holly leaves together by twisting the wires together. Join two or three holly berries together and twist them around the pair of holly leaves. Add the primroses and ivy.

Tie the ribbon into a bow, and glue it to the back of the candle.

19
Three
Christmas
ducks

These three Christmas ducks would
look perfect on a mantelpiece.
They are made in exactly
the same way as the ducks out
for a walk (see page 44).
The Christmas ducks are decorated
in cheery festive colours, and come
carrying gifts.
Actual size: Large duck 75mm
(3in), medium 64mm (2½in),
small 50mm (2in)

DOUGHCRAFT

Salt dough

170g (6oz) plain flour

75g (3oz) table salt

75ml (3fl oz or ⅓ cup) water

You will need:

Cocktail stick

64mm (2½in) round cutter

20mm (¾in) round cutter

Green, yellow, red, white and black paints

Making the large duck

Roll some dough into a golf-size ball and gently press it down on a work surface to flatten the bottom.

Pinch out one side of the ball into a tail shape with your finger and thumb.

Make the feet from two small flattened balls. Join the feet to the body leaving a small space between each foot. Make some markings on the top of the feet to make them look webbed.

Roll a table tennis-size ball of dough and join it to the body. Roll a small ball of dough for the beak and join it to the head. Cut the beak in half to separate the top and bottom. Make the eyes using the point of a cocktail stick.

To make the wings, roll two small balls of dough and flatten them between your finger and thumb. Pinch one end of each flattened ball out to form a wing. Join the wings to the body. Make some feather-like markings with a knife.

Roll out some dough so that it is 13mm (½in) thick and cut an oblong shape measuring 13 x 20mm (½ x ¾in). Roll a thin rope of dough and join it in the form of a cross around the present. Join the present to the body, pressing the wings close.

To make a hat, roll a large marble-size ball of dough. Pinch and roll one end of the ball. Put your finger into the opposite end of the ball making a well, pulling out the edge. Fold over the narrow end and secure it with a little water. Make a small pompom for the end of the hat.

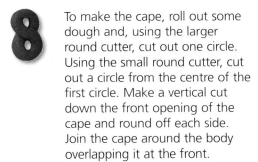

8 To make the cape, roll out some dough and, using the larger round cutter, cut out one circle. Using the small round cutter, cut out a circle from the centre of the first circle. Make a vertical cut down the front opening of the cape and round off each side. Join the cape around the body overlapping it at the front.

9 Roll a thin rope of dough. Join the rope to the edge of the cape. Rough up the surface of the rope using the point of a knife. Join the hat to the head. Roll a very thin rope of dough and join it to the edge of the hat. Rough up the surface of the rope using the point of a knife.

10 To make the medium and small ducks, follow the instructions as for large duck, making each one smaller than the last. Place the ducks onto a baking tray and bake at temperature 110°C (220°F or Gas Mark ¼) for about four hours.

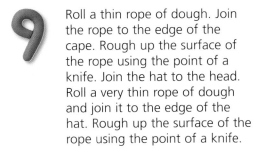

Finishing the Christmas ducks

11 Once the ducks have cooled, you can paint them.
- Green, purple, yellow, pink, red and blue, for the presents
- Yellow, for the feet and beaks
- Bright red, for the capes and hats
- White, for the head, body, wings, pompom and fur trimmings
- Black, for the eyes

When the paint is dry, apply two coats of varnish.

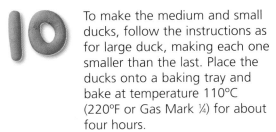

20
Santa
Claus

Christmas just wouldn't be
complete without Santa Claus.
This Santa has a soft body, made
from material and stuffed, just like
a soft toy. The head, arms and legs
are all made from salt dough.
Don't be put off by the fact that
the body needs to be sewn
together, only the most basic
stitches are required.
Actual size: Height 200mm (8in)

DOUGHCRAFT

Salt dough

50g (2oz) plain four

25g (1oz) table salt

25ml (1fl oz or ⅛ cup) water

You will need:

2 small black beads, for the eyes

Hairpin cut to 25mm (1in)

Strong sewing thread and needle

Cocktail stick

Fast-setting glue

Kitchen foil

Small hole drinking straw

200mm (8in) fabric, for the body

Small amount fibre filling to stuff the body

240 x 300mm (9½ x 12in) red felt fabric, for Santa's suit and hat

915mm (1 yard) fur trim, 13mm (½in) wide, for Santa's suit and hat

Making the head, arms and legs

Roll a large marble-size ball of dough for the head. Make the cheeks from two pea-size balls and flatten them. Smooth the edges of the cheeks with a paintbrush. Roll a small ball for the nose and join it between the cheeks. Make two holes for the eyes with the point of a cocktail stick and push a bead into each eyehole.

 Push the hairpin in at the lower part of the head under the chin, and lay it on a baking tray. Make a small circle of crumpled kitchen foil, and place it around the head to stop it from rolling around.

 To make the arms and mittens, roll a finger rope of dough about 126mm (5in) long. Cut the rope in half and round off one end of each piece with your finger and thumb. Flatten the ends slightly to make the hands. Cut a notch for the thumbs using the knife. Make a hole 6mm (¼in) in at the top of each arm with the drinking straw.

 To make the legs and boots, roll a finger rope of dough about 160mm (6½in) long and cut it in half. Make a hole 6mm (¼in) from the top of each leg with the drinking straw. Round off the end of each leg to make the boot.

 Put the legs and arms on a baking tray with the head and bake at 100°C (200°F or Gas Mark ¼) for about five hours. After the dough has cooled, add some fast-setting glue to keep the hairpin at the bottom of the head in place.

 Thread some sewing cotton through the hole of the hairpin and the holes in the arms and legs. Make loops to hang each piece up with.

Finishing the head, arms and legs

 Hang the head, arms and legs up so they are easier to paint and varnish.
- Black, for legs and boots
- Brown, for the arms and mittens
- Watery red, for Santa's nose
- White, for Santa's eyebrows
Apply two coats of varnish.

Making the soft body

Fold the cotton fabric in half and cut two rectangles measuring 90 x 115mm (3½ x 4½in). Stitch three sides of the rectangles together, leaving a seam of 6mm (¼in). The side which is open is the top of the body.

Turn the fabric so that the seam is inside, and stuff the body with the fibre filling. Stitch the shoulder seams together leaving a 13mm (½in) opening in the top of the body.

Assembling the body, head, legs and arms

Using doubled-up thread, sew through the holes in the salt dough and make a few firm stitches in the body to attach them.

Using doubled-up thread again, make a few stitches, one on top of the other, in the centre back of the body. Push the needle into the back of the body and bring it up through the 13mm (½in) opening at the top. Thread the needle through the hairpin on the head, and push it down into the neck opening and out through the centre back of the body (keep the thread loose at this stage).

Put a few drops of fast-setting glue around the hairpin under the head and pull the thread at the back of the body tight, pushing the head and body firmly together. Hold for 30 seconds. The head should now be firmly attached to the body. Make a few casting off stitches and cut the thread.

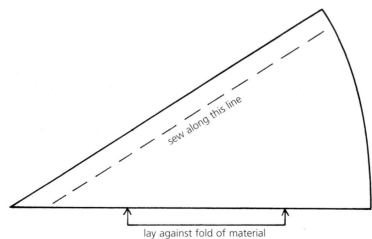

sew along this line

lay against fold of material

Making the Santa suit and hat

 Make a copy of the Santa suit and hat patterns and use them to cut out the red felt material. Stitch or glue the suit together leaving a 6mm (¼in) seam.

 Remember to leave openings for the neck, arms and legs. Cut a 50mm (2in) opening in the middle of one side of the suit. Put the suit on Santa and stitch the front opening together.

 Cut the fur trim into strips and glue them around the arms, legs, waist and at the front of the suit.

 Stitch the hat together. Put some glue around the top of Santa's head and attach the hat. Glue a strip of fur trim around the bottom edge of the hat. Cut a small piece of fur trim and glue this to the end of the hat as a pompom.

 Cut a small piece of fur trim for Santa's beard and moustache and glue them in place.

SANTA CLAUS

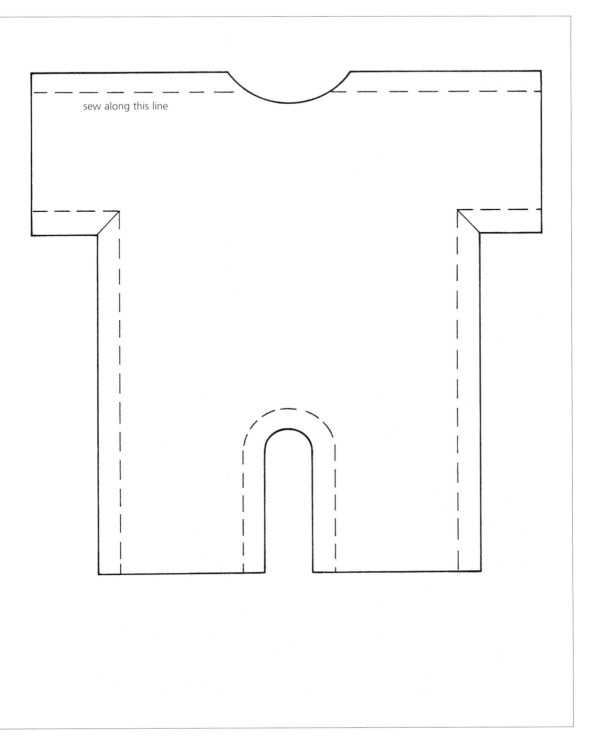

sew along this line

About the author

Patricia Hughes has followed a career as an accomplished interior designer, possessing many qualifications in this subject. She has always had a creative mind and has explored many other aspects of art.

This is her first published book in which she hopes that her unique creative flair will inspire readers to take up this wonderful craft.

GMC PUBLICATIONS

Books

rafts

nerican Patchwork Designs in Needlepoint	Melanie Tacon
Beginners' Guide to Rubber Stamping	Brenda Hunt
ltic Knotwork Designs	Sheila Sturrock
ltic Knotwork Handbook	Sheila Sturrock
llage from Seeds, Leaves and Flowers	Joan Carver
mplete Pyrography	Stephen Poole
eating Knitwear Designs	Pat Ashforth & Steve Plummer
eative Doughcraft	Patricia Hughes
eative Embroidery Techniques	
Jsing Colour Through Gold	Daphne J. Ashby & Jackie Woolsey
oss Stitch Kitchen Projects	Janet Granger
oss Stitch on Colour	Sheena Rogers
signing and Making Cards	Glennis Gilruth
nbroidery Tips & Hints	Harold Hayes
n Introduction to Crewel Embroidery	Mave Glenny
aking Character Bears	Valerie Tyler
aking Greetings Cards for Beginners	Pat Sutherland
aking Hand-Sewn Boxes: Techniques and Projects	Jackie Woolsey
aking Knitwear Fit	Pat Ashforth & Steve Plummer
edlepoint: A Foundation Course	Sandra Hardy
rography Designs	Norma Gregory
rography Handbook (Practical Crafts)	Stephen Poole
bbons and Roses	Lee Lockhead
ssel Making for Beginners	Enid Taylor
tting Collage	Lindsay Rogers
mari: A Traditional Japanese Embroidery Technique	Margaret Ludlow
eatre Models in Paper and Card	Robert Burgess
ool Embroidery and Design	Lee Lockhead

olls' Houses and Miniatures

chitecture for Dolls' Houses	Joyce Percival
ginners' Guide to the Dolls' House Hobby	Jean Nisbett
e Complete Dolls' House Book	Jean Nisbett
e Dolls' House 1/24 Scale: A Complete Introduction	Jean Nisbett
olls' House Accessories, Fixtures and Fittings	Andrea Barham
olls' House Bathrooms: Lots of Little Loos	Patricia King
olls' House Fireplaces and Stoves	Patricia King
sy to Make Dolls' House Accessories	Andrea Barham
eraldic Miniature Knights	Peter Greenhill
ake Your Own Dolls' House Furniture	Maurice Harper
aking Dolls' House Furniture	Patricia King
aking Georgian Dolls' Houses	Derek Rowbottom
aking Miniature Gardens	Freida Gray
aking Miniature Oriental Rugs & Carpets	Meik & Ian McNaughton
aking Period Dolls' House Accessories	Andrea Barham
aking Period Dolls' House Furniture	Derek & Sheila Rowbottom
aking Tudor Dolls' Houses	Derek Rowbottom
aking Unusual Miniatures	Graham Spalding
aking Victorian Dolls' House Furniture	Patricia King
iniature Bobbin Lace	Roz Snowden
iniature Embroidery for the Victorian Dolls' House	Pamela Warner
iniature Needlepoint Carpets	Janet Granger
e Secrets of the Dolls' House Makers	Jean Nisbett

Woodcarving

The Art of the Woodcarver	GMC Publications
Carving Birds & Beasts	GMC Publications
Carving on Turning	Chris Pye
Carving Realistic Birds	David Tippey
Decorative Woodcarving	Jeremy Williams
Essential Tips for Woodcarvers	GMC Publications
Essential Woodcarving Techniques	Dick Onians
Lettercarving in Wood: A Practical Course	Chris Pye
Power Tools for Woodcarving	David Tippey
Practical Tips for Turners & Carvers	GMC Publications
Relief Carving in Wood: A Practical Introduction	Chris Pye
Understanding Woodcarving	GMC Publications
Understanding Woodcarving in the Round	GMC Publications
Useful Techniques for Woodcarvers	GMC Publications
Wildfowl Carving – Volume 1	Jim Pearce
Wildfowl Carving – Volume 2	Jim Pearce
The Woodcarvers	GMC Publications
Woodcarving: A Complete Course	Ron Butterfield
Woodcarving: A Foundation Course	Zoë Gertner
Woodcarving for Beginners	GMC Publications
Woodcarving Tools & Equipment Test Reports	GMC Publications
Woodcarving Tools, Materials & Equipment	Chris Pye

Woodturning

Adventures in Woodturning	David Springett
Bert Marsh: Woodturner	Bert Marsh
Bill Jones' Notes from the Turning Shop	Bill Jones
Bill Jones' Further Notes from the Turning Shop	Bill Jones
Colouring Techniques for Woodturners	Jan Sanders
The Craftsman Woodturner	Peter Child
Decorative Techniques for Woodturners	Hilary Bowen
Essential Tips for Woodturners	GMC Publications
Faceplate Turning	GMC Publications
Fun at the Lathe	R.C. Bell
Illustrated Woodturning Techniques	John Hunnex
Intermediate Woodturning Projects	GMC Publications
Keith Rowley's Woodturning Projects	Keith Rowley
Make Money from Woodturning	Ann & Bob Phillips
Multi-Centre Woodturning	Ray Hopper
Pleasure and Profit from Woodturning	Reg Sherwin
Practical Tips for Turners & Carvers	GMC Publications
Practical Tips for Woodturners	GMC Publications
Spindle Turning	GMC Publications
Turning Miniatures in Wood	John Sainsbury
Turning Wooden Toys	Terry Lawrence
Understanding Woodturning	Ann & Bob Phillips
Useful Techniques for Woodturners	GMC Publications
Useful Woodturning Projects	GMC Publications
Woodturning: Bowls, Platters, Hollow Forms, Vases, Vessels, Bottles, Flasks, Tankards, Plates	GMC Publications
Woodturning: A Foundation Course	Keith Rowley
Woodturning: A Source Book of Shapes	John Hunnex
Woodturning Jewellery	Hilary Bowen
Woodturning Masterclass	Tony Boase
Woodturning Techniques	GMC Publications
Woodturning Tools & Equipment Test Reports	GMC Publications
Woodturning Wizardry	David Springett

Woodworking

40 More Woodworking Plans & Projects	GMC Publications
Bird Boxes and Feeders for the Garden	Dave Mackenzie
Complete Woodfinishing	Ian Hosker
David Charlesworth's Furniture-Making Techniques	David Charlesworth
Electric Woodwork	Jeremy Broun
Furniture & Cabinetmaking Projects	GMC Publications
Furniture Projects	Rod Wales
Furniture Restoration (Practical Crafts)	Kevin Jan Bonner
Furniture Restoration and Repair for Beginners	Kevin Jan Bonner
Furniture Restoration Workshop	Kevin Jan Bonner
Green Woodwork	Mike Abbott
The Incredible Router	Jeremy Broun
Making & Modifying Woodworking Tools	Jim Kingshott
Making Chairs and Tables	GMC Publications
Making Fine Furniture	Tom Darby
Making Little Boxes from Wood	John Bennett
Making Shaker Furniture	Barry Jackson
Making Woodwork Aids and Devices	Robert Wearing
Pine Furniture Projects for the Home	Dave Mackenzie
Router Magic: Jigs, Fixtures and Tricks to Unleash your Router's Full Potential	Bill Hylton
Routing for Beginners	Anthony Bailey
The Scrollsaw: Twenty Projects	John Everett
Sharpening Pocket Reference Book	Jim Kingshott
Sharpening: The Complete Guide	Jim Kingshott
Space-Saving Furniture Projects	Dave Mackenzie
Stickmaking: A Complete Course	Andrew Jones & Clive George
Stickmaking Handbook	Andrew Jones & Clive George
Test Reports: The Router and Furniture & Cabinetmaking	GMC Publications
Veneering: A Complete Course	Ian Hosker
Woodfinishing Handbook (Practical Crafts)	Ian Hosker
Woodworking Plans and Projects	GMC Publications
Woodworking with the Router: Professional Router Techniques any Woodworker can Use	Bill Hylton & Fred Matlack
The Workshop	Jim Kingshott

Upholstery

Seat Weaving (Practical Crafts)	Ricky Holdstock
The Upholsterer's Pocket Reference Book	David James
Upholstery: A Complete Course	David James
Upholstery Restoration	David James
Upholstery Techniques & Projects	David James

Toymaking

Designing & Making Wooden Toys	Terry Kelly
Fun to Make Wooden Toys & Games	Jeff & Jennie Loader
Making Board, Peg & Dice Games	Jeff & Jennie Loader
Making Wooden Toys & Games	Jeff & Jennie Loader
Restoring Rocking Horses	Clive Green & Anthony Dew
Scrollsaw Toy Projects	Ivor Carlyle
Wooden Toy Projects	GMC Publications

Home & Garden

Home Ownership: Buying and Maintaining	Nicholas Snelling
The Living Tropical Greenhouse	John and Maureen Tampion
Security for the Householder: Fitting Locks and Other Devices	E. Phillips

Videos

Drop-in and Pinstuffed Seats	David James
Stuffover Upholstery	David James
Elliptical Turning	David Springett
Woodturning Wizardry	David Springett
Turning Between Centres: The Basics	Dennis White
Turning Bowls	Dennis White
Boxes, Goblets and Screw Threads	Dennis White
Novelties and Projects	Dennis White
Classic Profiles	Dennis White
Twists and Advanced Turning	Dennis White
Sharpening the Professional Way	Jim Kingshott
Sharpening Turning & Carving Tools	Jim Kingshott
Bowl Turning	John Jordan
Hollow Turning	John Jordan
Woodturning: A Foundation Course	Keith Rowley
Carving a Figure: The Female Form	Ray Gonzalez
The Router: A Beginner's Guide	Alan Goodsell
The Scroll Saw: A Beginner's Guide	John Burke

Magazines

Woodturning ◆ Woodcarving ◆ Furniture & Cabinetmaking
The Dolls' House Magazine ◆ Creative Crafts for the home
The Router ◆ The ScrollSaw ◆ BusinessMatters

The above represents a full list of all titles currently published or scheduled to be published.
All are available direct from the Publishers or through bookshops, newsagents and specialist
retailers. To place an order, or to obtain a complete catalogue, contact:

**GMC Publications,
Castle Place, 166 High Street, Lewes,
East Sussex BN7 1XU, United Kingdom
Tel: 01273 488005 Fax: 01273 478606**

Orders by credit card are accepted